THE CIRCULATORY SYSTEM

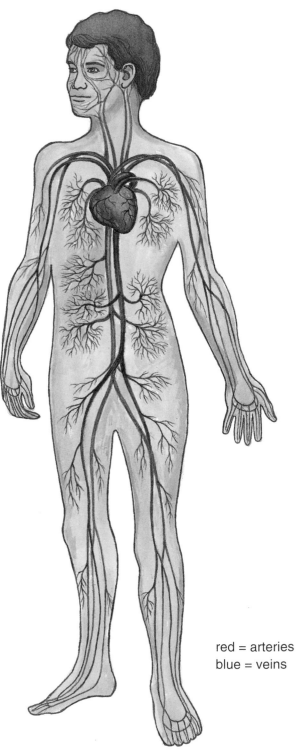

red = arteries
blue = veins

The Circulatory System

THE CIRCULATORY SYSTEM

DR. ALVIN, VIRGINIA, AND ROBERT SILVERSTEIN

TWENTY-FIRST CENTURY BOOKS
A Division of Henry Holt and Company
New York

Twenty-First Century Books
A Division of Henry Holt and Company, Inc.
115 West 18th Street
New York, NY 10011

Henry Holt ® and colophon are trademarks of
Henry Holt and Company, Inc.
Publishers since 1866

Published in Canada by Fitzhenry & Whiteside Ltd.
195 Allstate Parkway, Markham, Ontario L3R 4T8

Library of Congress Cataloging-in-Publication Data
Silverstein, Alvin.
Circulatory system / Alvin, Virginia, and Robert Silverstein. — 1st ed.
p.   cm. — (Human body systems)
Includes index.
1. Cardiovascular system—Juvenile literature. [1. Circulatory system.]
I. Silverstein, Virginia B. II. Silverstein, Robert A. III. Title. IV. Series.
QP103.S55 1994

612.1—dc20   94-21426
                                                                   CIP
                                                                   AC

First Edition 1994

Printed in Mexico
ISBN 0-8050-2833-1
All first editions are printed on acid-free paper∞.
10 9 8 7 6 5 4 3 2 1

Drawings by Lloyd Birmingham

Photo Credits

Cover: Howard Sochurek/The Stock Market, Inc.

p. 9: David Bassett/Photo Researchers, Inc.; p. 15 (tl): NMSB/Custom Medical Stock Photo; pp. 15 (br), 16 (tl and tr): Science Photo Library/Photo Researchers, Inc.; p. 16 (bl): North Wind Picture Archives; p. 16 (br): UPI/Bettmann; p. 27: B.S.I.P./Custom Medical Stock Photo; p. 30: Biophoto Associates/Science Source/Photo Researchers, Inc.; p. 36: Glauberman/Photo Researchers, Inc.; p. 41: Richard Hutchings/Photo Researchers, Inc.; p. 45: Bill Longcore/Science Source/Photo Researchers, Inc.; p. 53: Biology Media/Photo Researchers, Inc.; p. 56: Andy Levin/Photo Researchers, Inc.; p. 61: Junebug Clark/Photo Researchers, Inc.; p. 63: Yvonne Hemsey/Gamma Liaison; p. 64: Gary Retherford/Photo Researchers, Inc.; p. 69: Gower Med. Publ./Biophoto Associates/Photo Researchers, Inc.; pp. 73, 77 (l): SIU/Photo Researchers, Inc.; p. 75 Montagnier/Institute Pasteur/SPL/Photo Researchers, Inc.; pp. 77 (r), 82: Mehau Kulyk/Science Photo Library/Photo Researchers, Inc.; p. 81: Will and Deni McIntyre/Photo Researchers, Inc.; p. 85: Mitsuhiro Wata/Gamma; p. 87: Randy Taylor/ICS/The Gamma Liaison Network

CONTENTS

SECTION 1

BLOOD FOR LIFE

Inside us there is a pump that never stops working as long as we live. It is the heart, and it pumps a red liquid called **blood** to nearly every part of our bodies, through a system of tubes called **blood vessel**s. The blood circulates around the body over and over again, which is why the heart and blood vessels are called the circulatory system.

The circulatory system is the body's highway system for transporting materials. It works closely with all of the other systems of the body. It helps the respiratory system deliver oxygen to the trillions of cells that make up our bodies, and it works with the excretory system to take away **carbon dioxide** and other waste products the cells don't need. It helps the digestive system deliver food materials that the cells can use as building blocks for growth and repair or can "burn" for energy to do their jobs. Without the steady supply of oxygen and food materials carried in the blood, the cells would die.

Blood also carries many other important substances. It helps deliver special chemical messengers called **hormones** that give instructions to tissues and organs. It carries germ-fighting chemicals called **antibodies**, too. White blood cells patrol the blood vessel highways like microscopic soldiers, ready to defend the body against invading germs and other threats. Chemicals in the blood help the body to heal injuries. Blood also carries heat from one part of the body to another and helps to keep the temperature inside us at a safe and normal level. Many of the body's chemical reactions take place in the watery blood.

The heart never rests, even when we are sleeping, and the bloodstream highways are always open, day and night, to keep us alive and healthy.

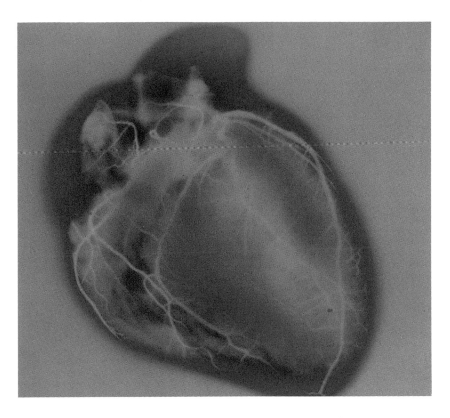

*X ray of the heart showing the arteries and veins
that supply blood to the cardiac muscles*

ANIMALS AND PLANTS

All living creatures, from tiny one-celled amebas to tall trees and huge whales, need supplies of food and oxygen and make waste products that must be taken away. Circulation of materials takes place in all of them. But not all have circulatory systems like ours.

Single-celled creatures such as the amebas that live in ponds are so small that no part of them is far from the water in which they live. They don't really need a circulatory system. Food particles can easily get to all parts of the cell by floating along in the cell fluid, and wastes pass out through the cell's outer membrane into the surrounding water. Flatworms, although they grow only as big as the tip of your thumb, are made up of millions of cells. But a flatworm is so flat that none of its cells is very far from the surface. It, too, can get along without a real circulatory system.

Most animals have thicker and larger bodies, though, and most of their cells are buried deep within many layers of other cells. In these animals, a circulatory system, in which blood flows throughout the body, helps meet the needs of all the cells.

In some animals, blood flows through a simple network of tubes and hollow spaces. This arrangement is called an open circulatory system, because the blood flows in open spaces. Simple animals like the ribbon worm do not have a pump to force blood around the body. Their body movements are all that keeps the blood flowing.

In some animals, blood is pumped around the body when blood vessels (or special portions of them, called pumping centers) contract. Grasshoppers and other insects, for example, have a single blood vessel down the length of the back. A series of pumping centers at the end act as a heart to pump blood into hollow spaces. Blood passes slowly through the

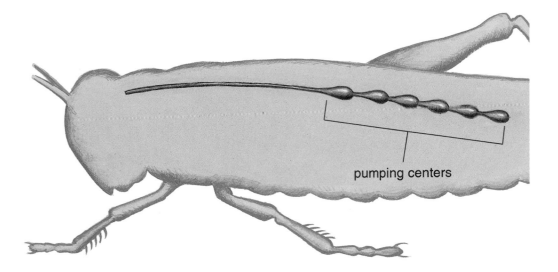

pumping centers

A grasshopper has a very simple system for
pumping blood into hollow spaces in its body.

hollow spaces past all the organs of the insect's body and back to the "heart."

The vertebrates—mammals, birds, reptiles, and amphibians—have closed circulatory systems. Blood remains inside a network of blood vessels and is pumped through the body by a heart. Oxygen and food materials pass out of the tiniest of the vessels and into the cells.

The hearts of all vertebrates are made of muscle tissue. But the structure of the heart is very different in the different groups of vertebrates.

Fish and amphibian hearts have a single pump to keep blood flowing. A fish heart is divided into two chambers, and amphibian hearts have three chambers. These circulatory systems are not very efficient. The four-chambered heart of birds and mammals works much better. Bird and mammal hearts are actually two pumps. One sends the blood from the cells to the lungs to pick up oxygen, and the other pumps oxygen-rich blood to the cells.

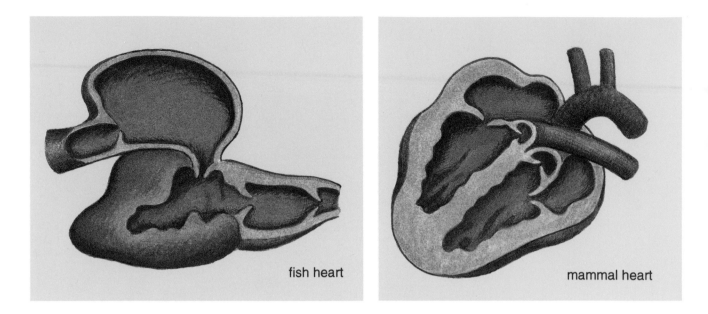

A fish heart has two chambers, while a mammal heart has four.

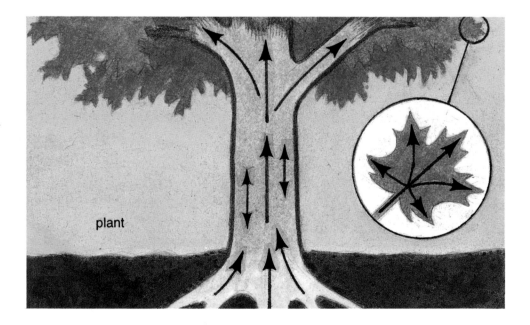

A plant has a very efficient circulatory system without a pump. Water evaporates through tiny openings in the leaves called stomata, creating a suction that pulls water to the top of the plant. Food manufactured by the leaves flows throughout the plant.

Plants do not have hearts or pumps. But even trees that are hundreds of feet tall can deliver water and salts to cells all the way at the top. A plant's circulatory system is made up of many thin tubes. Xylem vessels carry water and salts from the roots up to the leaves. Sugars and other foods manufactured by the leaves are carried up or down through tubes called phloem vessels. What makes water flow up against gravity? Water evaporates into the air through tiny holes (called stomata) in the leaves. This creates a suction, pulling more fluid up to take the place of the water that left.

LEARNING ABOUT THE CIRCULATORY SYSTEM

In almost every culture people have thought of the heart and blood as essential to life. The ancient Greeks believed that the soul was carried in the blood. Some early religions taught that sickness was caused by evil spirits in the blood. The Bible says that blood is life.

About 3,600 years ago, Egyptian doctors knew that vessels went from the heart to all parts of the body. But they didn't know that blood traveled through those vessels. The ancient Egyptians thought that the heart was where a person's thoughts and feelings came from.

Chinese doctors who lived 3,000 years ago wrote that the heart controlled the flow of blood through blood vessels. But they believed the blood vessels also carried other substances, such as air and urine.

Greek scientists in the fifth century B.C. thought that a special kind of air flowed through the blood vessels and was the spirit of life. A century later, Herophilus pointed out that veins and arteries were very different. He also showed that blood, not air, flowed through veins. Another Greek physician, Erasistratos, noted 2,300 years ago that every organ in the body had a vein and an artery leading to it. He agreed that veins carried blood, but he insisted that air flowed in the arteries. (The word *artery* means "air carrier.")

In the second century A.D., the Greek physician Galen showed that arteries carried blood, not air. But he had a lot of mistaken ideas, too. Galen thought that the heart worked like an oven to keep blood warm, and that blood flowed back and forth like the tides in the ocean. He said the liver was the center of the circulatory system. Galen's ideas were held as truth for nearly 1,400 years. Some people were killed for doubting them.

In medieval times it was thought that diseases were caused by blood that had become stagnant. Barbers practiced bloodletting (purposely causing bleeding) to get the "bad blood" out and get the flow going better. Blood-feeding animals called leeches were also used to suck out blood. Unfortunately many people died from these treatments.

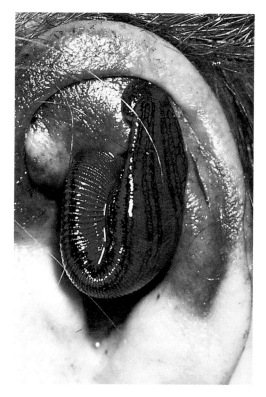

A leech produces a chemical substance called hirudin, which prevents blood from clotting. Today, doctors may use leeches to reduce the accumulation of blood after certain surgical procedures. Here, a leech is sucking blood to reduce swelling in an injured ear.

William Harvey

Several scientists made important discoveries about the heart and blood vessels during the sixteenth century, but it wasn't until the early seventeenth century that an English doctor named William Harvey figured out how the circulatory system really works. By studying the bodies of dead people and experimenting on living animals, he discovered that the heart is the pump that keeps blood

Marcello Malpighi

Stephen Hales

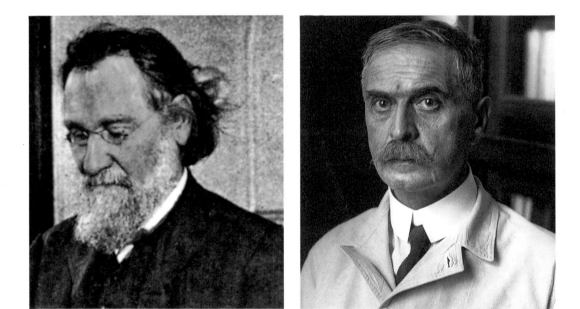

Elie Metchnikoff

Karl Landsteiner

moving, and that blood circulates through the blood vessels in a one-way flow, not back and forth.

In the 1660s an Italian doctor, Marcello Malpighi, saw tiny blood vessels that connected arteries and veins. He named them capillaries, from the Latin word for "hair," because they were smaller than the thinnest hairs. Malpighi had found the last link in the circle.

In the 1660s Dutch microscope maker Antonie van Leeuwenhoek saw red blood cells inside the capillaries of a tadpole's tail. In the mid-1700s an English scientist, Stephen Hales, described blood pressure. In the late 1800s, Russian scientist Elie Metchnikoff discovered disease-fighting white blood cells. In 1901 an Austrian doctor, Karl Landsteiner, discovered that humans have four different blood types. And during the past century, doctors have learned much about circulatory diseases and how to treat them.

OUR CIRCULATORY SYSTEM

If the blood vessels in our circulatory system were stretched out end to end, they would reach over 62,000 miles (nearly 100,000 kilometers). That's enough to go around the earth more than twice! Inside the body the blood vessels are linked into a complicated system. It takes less than a minute for the blood to circulate all around the body, and this happens about a thousand times a day.

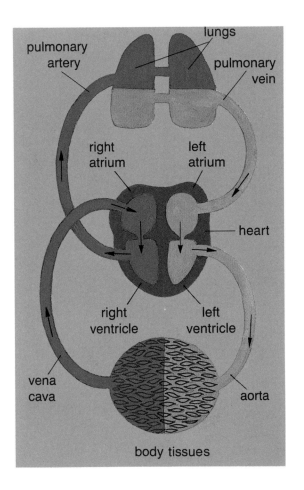

pulmonary artery · lungs · pulmonary vein · right atrium · left atrium · heart · right ventricle · left ventricle · vena cava · aorta · body tissues

We really have two circulatory systems. The **pulmonary circulation** is a short loop from the heart to the lungs and back again. The **systemic circulation** provides blood to all parts of the body. Both circuits start and end at the heart, but there is no mixing between them.

Blood flows away from the heart in thick, muscular blood vessels called **arteries**. These branch out into smaller and smaller vessels. The smallest arteries are called **arterioles**. They connect with even smaller blood vessels called **capillaries**. Capillaries are so small they can be seen only with a microscope. Nearly every living cell in the body has a capillary near it. Oxygen and other nutrients pass through the capillary walls into the cells. Waste products pass from the cells into the capillaries. These waste products are brought back to the heart as the capillaries join to form **venules**. As these venules get closer to the heart they become larger **veins**, which eventually empty into the heart.

There are blood vessels leading to all major organs and areas in the body. For each major artery carrying blood to an area there is usually a vein draining blood away from it.

Muscles make up about 40 percent of the body. Normally the muscles receive only 20 percent of the blood supply, though they get a lot more during exercise. The brain is a rather small organ compared to all the muscles, and yet the brain receives 25 percent of the blood supply!

Arteries carry blood with very little oxygen (**deoxygenated blood**) to the lungs. This blood also contains the cells' waste products, such as carbon dioxide. In the lungs, oxygen passes into the capillaries through their thin walls, and carbon dioxide passes out into the lungs' tiny air sacs, to be exhaled. Veins carry blood rich in oxygen (**oxygenated blood**) from the lungs back to the heart. Then arteries of the systemic circulation carry this freshly oxygenated blood from the heart to the cells of the body. The veins of the systemic system return deoxygenated blood to the heart.

Blood vessels are like plumbing in a house, except that blood vessels continually expand and contract with the rhythmic blood flow and the changing needs of the body. The force that keeps the blood moving is the steady beating of a powerful pump, the heart.

WHAT COLOR IS YOUR BLOOD?

Oxygen gives blood a bright red color. But deoxygenated blood is bluish purple. In the systemic circulation, arteries carry bright red, oxygenated blood and veins carry purplish, deoxygenated blood. (Remember, it is the reverse in the pulmonary circulation.) Why don't you bleed bluish purple blood when you cut yourself? Because oxygen from the air immediately oxygenates the blood that flows out of a cut vein.

THE STRUCTURE OF THE HEART

We speak of a heart full of love, of kindhearted people, of hearts that are pure, and hearts of stone. Our emotions and thoughts really come from the brain, but it isn't hard to see why people thought our feelings came from the heart—we can feel our hearts pounding when we are in love or when we're afraid, or full of any other emotion.

Your heart doesn't look like a valentine heart. It is a hollow muscle about the size and shape of your fist. It is not on your left side, either, as most people think. Your heart lies between your lungs, in a slanting position in the center of your chest behind your rib cage. The top is wider and points to the right. The narrower end points downward toward the left, closer to the ribs. That is where we hear the heart beating, which is why people think it is on the left.

A human heart has four chambers, but it can also be thought of as two hearts, each with two chambers. A muscular wall called a **septum** divides the two sides of the heart. Each side of the heart has a thin-walled upper chamber called an **atrium** (Latin for "entrance hall"). These atria are holding chambers for the blood entering the heart from the veins. Beneath each atrium is a larger chamber called a **ventricle** (Latin for "little belly"). The ventricles are the pumps, and their walls are thicker and more muscular than those of the atria.

Valves help to control the flow of blood through the heart. These valves let the blood go in only one direction. The **tricuspid valve** directs the flow of blood from the right atrium to the right ventricle. The **mitral valve** is between the left atrium and left ventricle. **Semilunar valves** control the flow from ventricles to the arteries.

The working part of the heart is its muscular wall. It is made up of three layers. The outer protective layer is a thin, shiny membrane called the epi-

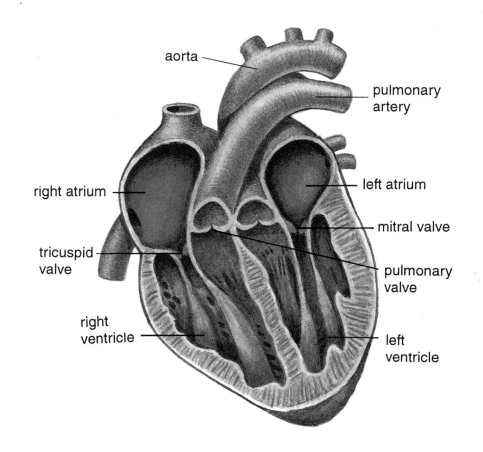

A cross section showing the main chambers and valves of the heart

cardium. The main layer is the **cardiac muscle**, also called the **myocardium**. Unlike other muscles in the body, cardiac muscle doesn't get tired. The **endocardium** lines the inside of the heart and protects it from irritation by the blood constantly swirling around inside.

These heart tissues need a lot of oxygen to do their work. This is supplied by the **coronary arteries**, which stretch over the outside walls of the heart in a complicated network.

The heart is packaged in a thin sac called the **pericardium** (Latin for "around the heart"). This protective covering keeps the heart from rubbing against the lungs and the chest wall.

FORMATION OF THE
FETAL HEART

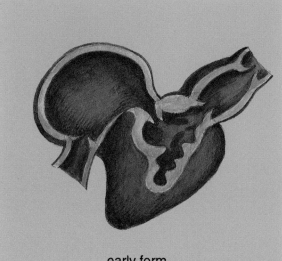

early form
similar to fish heart

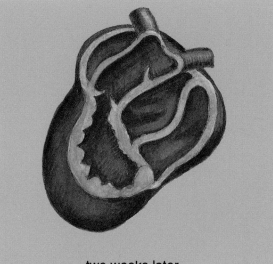

two weeks later
similar to frog heart

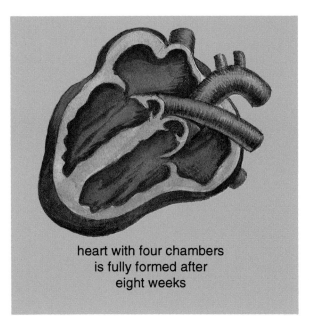

heart with four chambers
is fully formed after
eight weeks

HOW YOUR HEART FORMED

Your heart started beating about eight months before you were born. At first it was a simple tube. Then an atrium and a ventricle began to take shape, and your heart was two-chambered, like that of a fish. At five weeks of life, you had a three-chambered heart: the atria were partly separated, but the ventricles had no wall between them. This is like the heart of an amphibian, such as a frog. Next, the atria were separated, but the ventricles were only partly separated, and the heart resembled that of a reptile, such as a snake. Finally, the septum dividing the ventricles was complete, to form a four-chambered heart.

THE HEART IS A PUMP

Your heart pumps almost 2,000 gallons (7,500 liters) of blood around your body each day. That's about 50 million gallons in your lifetime. The heart pumps blood by constantly contracting (squeezing) and relaxing. It does this an average of 70 times each minute—more than 100,000 times each day. Each cycle is a **heartbeat**, and during an average lifetime the heart beats 2.5 billion times.

When the heart beats, the muscles at the top (the atria) contract first, and then the ventricles contract. But this happens so quickly that the heart seems to be contracting all at once. After each contraction, both chambers rest. So although the heart is always working, it really rests for nearly half the time. The contracting part of the heartbeat cycle is called the **systole**. The relaxing part is called the **diastole.**

With every heartbeat, both the left and right sides of the heart contract and relax. Each time the left ventricle relaxes, the chamber becomes larger, and blood filled with oxygen flows down into it from the left atrium. Each time it contracts or squeezes, the oxygen-filled blood is squirted into the **aorta**, which leads out into thousands of smaller arteries to carry the oxygen-rich blood all over the body.

The right ventricle also squeezes and relaxes, but not as hard. It pushes carbon-dioxide-carrying blood out through the **pulmonary trunk**, which leads to the lungs. The left side has to work harder than the right to pump the blood to the farthest parts of the body. That's why the walls of the left ventricle are three times as thick as the right ventricle.

The "lub, dub" sound we hear when the heart beats is the sound of the valves closing. The contraction of the heart (systole) is followed by closing of the valves between the atria and ventricles—which makes the "lub" sound. After the heart relaxes, the valves between the ventricles and the arteries snap shut—the "dub" sound.

Sometimes a doctor may hear a hissing or shushing sound between the lub, dub sounds. These sounds are called **heart murmurs**. There are many possible reasons for murmurs. Usually they are just the sound of blood rushing through the heart, and are perfectly normal. But sometimes a heart murmur can be a sign of a serious problem, one that a person was born with or that was caused by an illness. For example, the sound might be due to a leaking valve that lets extra blood get through when the valve is closed.

THE STAGES OF A HEARTBEAT

1. Diastole: Oxygen–rich blood from the lungs enters the relaxed left atrium and flows into the relaxed left ventricle; deoxygenated blood from the body flows into the relaxed right atrium and ventricle.

2. Systole:

a. The atria contract, sending more blood through valves into the ventricles. The semilunar valves close so that blood cannot flow back from the arteries.

b. The ventricles start to contract and the atrial valves close so that blood cannot back up into the atria.

c. The ventricles finish contracting, pumping blood through the semilunar valves into the main arteries.

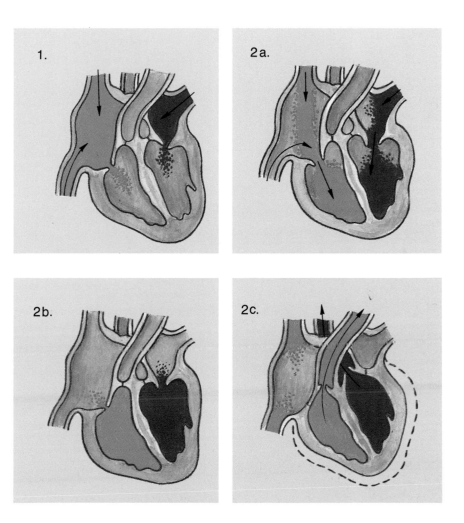

THE HEARTBEAT

Usually the heartbeat is very regular, like the ticking of a clock. A new-born baby's heart beats about 120 times each minute. As we grow older, our heartbeat slows down. A child's heartbeat rate might be from 80 to 100 times a minute, and an adult's heart beats an average of 70 times a minute. Women's hearts usually beat faster than men's.

You have probably felt your heartbeat speed up after you have been running or exercising. It feels as though your heart is pounding in your chest. The heartbeat rate can double during exercise. Your body needs to circulate the blood faster than normal to provide the muscles with extra energy. The heart can pump six to eight times as much blood during exercise as it pumps while you are resting. Fever, fear, and excitement and some drugs like caffeine and cocaine can make the heart beat faster, too.

Your heartbeat slows down while you are sleeping. People who have trained for running or other sports have slower heartbeats than the average. Exercise strengthens the heart, so the heart of a person who exercises regularly can pump more blood in each beat. Athletes' hearts may need to beat only 50 times a minute or even less during rest. (They speed up during exercise, but not as much as the average person's does.)

You can listen to a friend's heartbeat by putting your ear against the friend's chest. Each "lub, dub" you hear is one heartbeat. Doctors use a sound-magnifying instrument called a stethoscope to listen to the heart.

Another way to find out how fast your heart is beating is by taking your **pulse**. During each heartbeat the left ventricle pumps oxygen-rich blood into the aorta and out into the arteries of the body. The pressure on the flexible walls of the aorta creates a pressure wave that sweeps through the arteries like the ripples a rock makes when you throw it into the water. This pressure wave causes the arteries to expand, then contract, producing the

ANIMAL HEARTBEAT RATES

Mouse 650/min

Hamster 450/min

Iguana 150/min

Woodchuck 80/min

Duck, just after flight 540/min

Hamster, hibernating 4/min

Cat 120/min

Woodchuck, hibernating 3/min

In general, small animals have faster heartbeat rates than large ones, but activity can make a big difference.

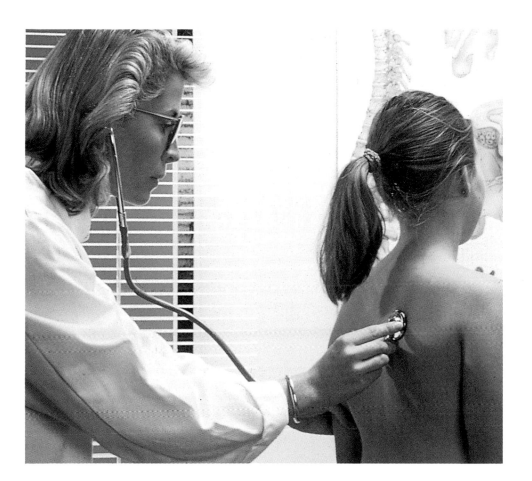

A doctor uses a stethoscope to listen to the heart and lungs.

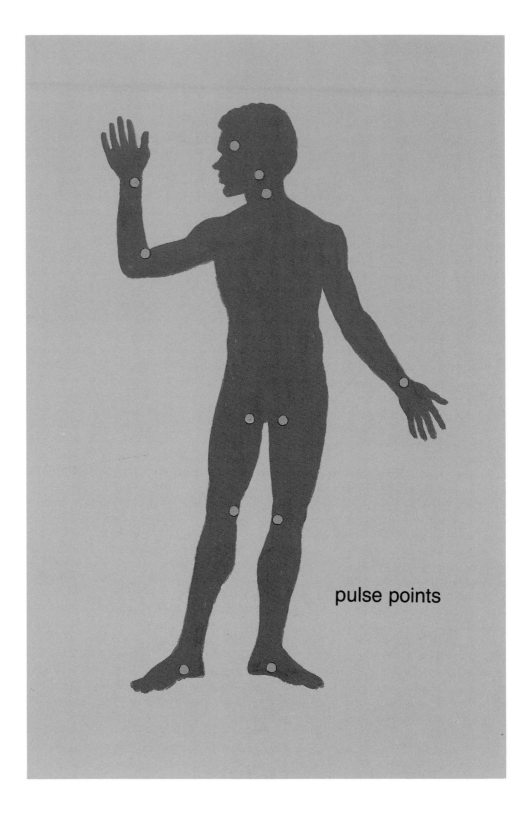

pulse points

rhythmic throbbing that is called the pulse. You can feel the pulse at places where arteries lie close to the surface of the skin. The inside of the wrist is the most common place to take a pulse. You can also feel a pulse in other arteries: in the temple, jaw, neck, arms, groin, instep, and behind the knee.

HOW TO TAKE A PULSE

Place the three middle fingers of one hand on the inside of your other wrist (on the side by the thumb) and press gently until you feel a regular throbbing. Look at the second hand of a clock or watch. Count the number of beats you feel in your wrist for exactly thirty seconds. Multiply the number of beats you have counted by two. That is your pulse rate. Each beat of the pulse is equal to the two sounds the heart makes during one heartbeat. (Never use your thumb to take someone's pulse. You have a pulse in your thumb, and you might mistakenly count that instead of the other person's pulse.)

REGULATING THE HEARTBEAT

What makes the heart beat? Heart muscle is different from the muscles that move our arms and legs. Those muscles do not contract unless a message from the brain, sent along a nerve, "tells" them to. But heart muscle can contract all by itself, without any messages from the nerves. In fact, if a heart is actually taken out of the body and placed in a warm solution with just the right amount of sugars and salts, it will continue to beat.

A special system of muscles in the heart causes the heart to beat with a regular rhythm. A heartbeat usually starts with a contraction of a small bit of tissue on the wall of the right atrium. This piece of tissue is called the **sinoatrial** or **S-A node**. It can contract like a muscle, but it can also send messages like a nerve. It is often called the "pacemaker" of the heart. It is like a built-in spark plug and timer. The pacemaker starts the heart contracting, sets the rate of the heartbeat, and keeps all the parts of the heart working to the same rhythm.

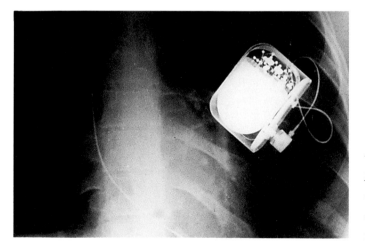

An X ray of an artificial pacemaker implanted in a patient's chest to help the heart maintain a regular rhythm

To start each heartbeat, the pacemaker sends out tiny bursts of electricity—not enough to cause a shock, but enough to start the heart muscle contracting. The electrical impulse passes through muscle cells of the atria to a second relay station, located between the atria and the ventricles. It is called the **atrioventricular** or **A-V node**. The impulse then travels through the septum separating the two ventricles and is sent to muscle cells in the right and left ventricles. It excites the muscles of the ventricles, which then pump blood into the arteries.

The body has several backup systems to make sure the flow of blood keeps up with the body's changing needs. These backup systems are like brakes and accelerators on a car, speeding up or slowing down the flow of blood, depending on what the body is doing. The pacemaker is connected by nerves to the brain and other parts of the body. Their messages may speed up or slow down the heartbeat, as when we are excited, or asleep, for example. People can even learn to speed up or slow down their heartbeat.

Various chemicals in the blood, such as carbon dioxide and hormones, also act on the pacemaker. When you are excited or frightened, your body makes a hormone called **adrenaline**. This chemical works through the pacemaker to make your heart speed up and pump blood faster through your body. This is your body's way of preparing you in case you may need to fight or run away.

CONTROLLING YOUR HEARTBEAT

Normally the heartbeat rate is controlled automatically, without any conscious thought. But people can learn to slow down their heartbeat by thinking of very calm and peaceful things. In biofeedback, special devices register the electrical activity of the heart and brain. A signal, such as a musical tone, sounds when the heart rate is slowing, and the person learns to recognize and produce the feelings that go with the slower pace.

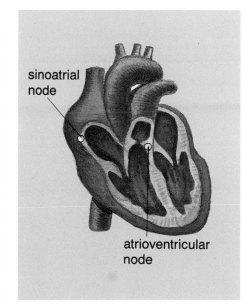

sinoatrial node

atrioventricular node

SECTION 2

Arteries

Veins

Capillaries

Blood Pressure

A Trip Around the Circulatory System

Blood

Blood Plasma

Red Blood Cells

White Blood Cells

The Immune System

ARTERIES

Arteries are the blood vessels that carry blood away from the heart. They have thick, muscular walls that are very flexible. The arteries' thick walls help them to keep their shape without collapsing after the surge of blood from each heartbeat has passed through.

Artery walls are made up of three layers. The working part of an artery is a layer of muscle and elastic tissue called the media. Protecting the outside of the artery is a tough, fibrous covering called the adventitia. On the inside is a slippery lining called the endothelium (intima) that keeps blood from leaking out of the artery.

Arteries bulge as each heartbeat sends blood gushing through them. After the blood passes by, the artery walls return to their normal shape, springing back like a stretched rubber band that is finally released. This helps give the blood another push to keep it moving along. (It is also the reason blood comes out in spurts when an artery is cut.) The contractions of the arteries and arterioles help to smooth out the flow, so that the rushing blood will not damage the delicate capillaries that bring nutrients to the body cells. At any one time, 15 percent of all the blood in the body is found in the arteries.

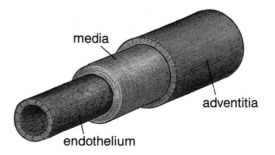

The media layer of an artery is elastic and lets the artery expand and contract with each heartbeat.

The largest artery in the body is the aorta. It is about an inch wide and shaped like the handle of a cane. The aorta curves up from the left ventricle and then down in front of the spine into the abdomen. Then it branches out into smaller and smaller arteries that deliver oxygen-rich blood to the body. Some of its main branches are shown in the diagram. Generally, arteries are named for the organ or body part they supply. The smallest arteries are called arterioles.

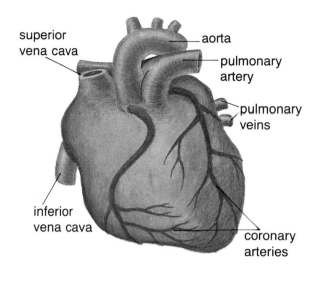

The heart has its own system of arteries and veins to keep it supplied with nourishment.

The pulmonary trunk is the other main artery of the circulatory system. Soon after leaving the right ventricle it divides into right and left branches, the **pulmonary arteries**, which deliver oxygen-poor blood to the lungs.

The heart needs a lot of energy to do its job. Even though it is filled with blood, the heart cannot use its own blood for nourishment. If there were blood vessels inside the chambers to feed the walls, they would be damaged when the blood was sent spurting through the heart. Also, the blood in the right side of the heart has very little oxygen, and it would not be able to supply the muscular walls there. Blood vessels on the outer surface of the heart, called the coronary arteries and coronary veins, satisfy its needs.

Two coronary arteries the size of drinking straws branch off at the beginning of the aorta and divide into a complicated network of small arteries across the surface of the heart. The smaller arteries eventually join each other. In this way, to some extent, if the blood supply to one area of the heart is stopped for some reason, other arteries may be able to supply it with the nutrients it needs to keep working.

The coronary arteries branch into capillaries inside the heart muscle. These capillaries join coronary veins to take away the heart's waste products. About 5 percent of all the blood the heart pumps is sent through the coronary arteries to supply itself. Arteries and veins have blood vessels to supply their nutrient needs, too.

VEINS

When you have blood tests done, or if you donate blood, the needle is usually inserted into a vein. It is much safer and simpler to take blood from a vein than from an artery. Arteries are usually found deep in the muscles, close to bones, where they are protected from injuries. When an artery is cut, blood gushes out in spurts, and large quantities can be lost quickly. The blood flow from a cut vein is much slower and steadier.

Veins have the same three-layered structure as arteries. But their walls are thinner and less flexible, and the middle muscle layer is much thinner than in the arteries. Unlike arteries, whose muscular walls help maintain their shape, veins tend to collapse if the pressure of the blood inside them drops. (Watch how the veins on the back of your hand flatten out when you raise your hand above the level of your heart.)

Veins carry cell wastes in the blood to either the lungs or to the kidneys. The smallest veins, called venules, begin at the capillaries and join into larger and larger veins as they approach the heart. The two largest veins are the **venae cavae**. The superior vena cava is just above the heart and the inferior vena cava just below.

One of the best-known veins is the **jugular vein** in the neck, which helps drain blood from the head. Some organs in the body, such as the liver, **spleen**, and bone marrow, have greatly enlarged vessels called **sinusoids**, which act as reser-

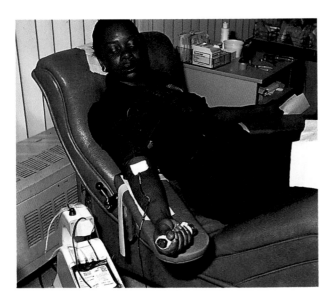

Donating blood is a simple and safe procedure.

voirs for blood. Greatly enlarged veins in the skull are called venous sinuses. At any given time, about 70 percent of the blood in the body can be found in the veins and sinusoids.

When you are lying down, blood can easily flow to the heart. But when you stand, blood must flow uphill against gravity in most of the body. This is not an easy task. The blood has slowed down during its passage through the arteries, arterioles, and capillaries. Blood pumped into the aorta travels at about 15 inches (40 centimeters) per second. By the time it reaches the capillaries it has slowed down to $\frac{1}{50}$ inch ($\frac{1}{20}$ centimeter) per second. And veins, unlike arteries, do not contract rhythmically to help blood flow along.

The skeletal muscles that surround veins support them and keep them from bulging. When you move, your muscles squeeze on your veins, helping blood to flow to the heart. The leg muscles thus act like a sort of pump. But if you stand perfectly still, the veins in your legs can become overfilled with blood, which leaks out into the surrounding tissue. As this pooling continues, less blood flows to the brain. After about fifteen minutes, lack of oxygen to the brain would cause you to topple over and faint. Soldiers standing at attention learn to tense their leg muscles every now and then to prevent this from happening. A faint is a self-correcting condition: as soon as you are in a horizontal position, the blood flows freely, and full circulation to the brain is restored.

Veins in the legs and arms and other parts of the body are equipped with valves. These valves help blood to flow uphill by preventing it from flowing backward once it has passed by. The valves are spaced every half-inch along the leg veins.

The rate at which the veins return blood to the heart helps to determine how much blood the heart pumps. Vigorous exercise can increase the heart's output from the normal 1.3 gallons (5 liters) to about 8 gallons (30 liters) per minute.

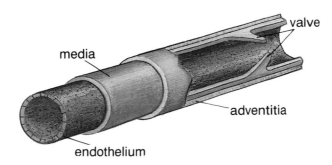

A vein, unlike an artery, has valves to keep the blood from flowing backward.

valve

media

adventitia

endothelium

CAPILLARIES

The purpose of all the pumping and transporting of blood is for the body's cells to exchange waste products for oxygen, glucose, and other essential substances. This transfer occurs across the tiny blood vessels called capillaries. Although they can only be seen with a microscope, capillaries can be thought of as the most important part of the circulatory system. The main function of the heart and large blood vessels is to deliver blood to and from the capillaries.

Capillaries are so tiny that it would take 25 of them laid end to end to equal one inch. And yet, because there are about 10 billion of them in the body, they make up 99 percent of the entire length of the circulatory system—about 62,000 miles (nearly 100,000 kilometers). But capillaries are less than $1/4{,}000$ inch (0.1 millimeter) wide—less than one-tenth the width of a hair. Not only do red blood cells (one of the smallest cells in the body) have to travel single file through the capillaries, but they have to squeeze to get through. The narrowness of the capillaries explains why they contain only 5 percent of the blood in the body.

Capillary walls are only one cell thick. Thin, curved cells called endothelial cells are joined together like a jigsaw puzzle. A thin layer of connective tissue gives the capillary support. Oxygen and other nutrients slip out between the cells in the capillary walls to the body cells. Carbon dioxide and other waste products pass from the cells through the capillary walls into the blood. This exchange takes place in a surprisingly short time: the blood spends only one to three seconds in a particular capillary before it flows on its way through the veins.

Capillaries are linked in intricate networks, and most cells in the body have a capillary close to them. These smallest blood vessels connect arterioles and venules together. Actually, it is often rather hard to tell where capillaries end and arterioles or venules begin. The venules only gradually

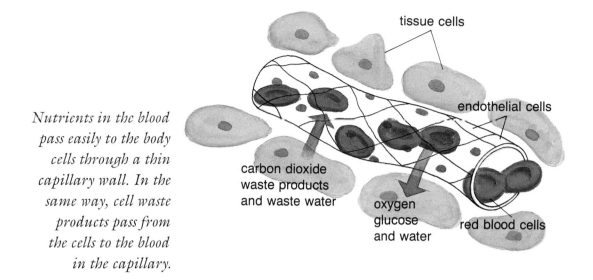

Nutrients in the blood pass easily to the body cells through a thin capillary wall. In the same way, cell waste products pass from the cells to the blood in the capillary.

tissue cells

endothelial cells

carbon dioxide waste products and waste water

oxygen glucose and water

red blood cells

acquire their three coats as they leave the capillary networks, and the arterioles change just as gradually as they merge with capillaries.

In some places, as in muscles and in the gastrointestinal tract, arterioles and venules are linked directly without any capillary networks. This helps the body shift blood to other areas. For example, during vigorous exercise the muscles receive 88 percent of the heart's output, while at rest they receive only 20 percent. During exertion the abdominal organs receive only 1 percent of the blood supply, but normally they get 24 percent of the heart output—and even more while they are digesting a meal. That is why it's not a good idea to exercise too soon after eating. So much of the blood is being diverted to the digestive organs that the muscles are starved.

CAPILLARIES FOR COLOR

People turn pale when they are frightened or cold because arterioles near the skin become narrower, cutting down the supply of blood that reaches the network of capillaries near the surface of the skin. Pinching the skin squeezes blood out of the capillaries, making the skin look white. When we blush or we're hot, the blood flow to the capillaries is increased, giving us rosy cheeks. The extra blood flowing through the skin gives off heat, helping to cool the body.

BLOOD PRESSURE

When blood is pumped out from the heart it rushes through the blood vessels, pressing on their walls as it passes by. This pressure is called **blood pressure**, and it can be measured in the arteries, veins, or capillaries. The blood pressure is not the same in the different blood vessels, though. So blood pressure is always measured in the same place—in the main artery in the arm.

The blood pressure is highest during the systole, when the heart is pumping a new spurt of blood into the arteries. As the wave of blood goes by, the pressure drops. During the diastole, when the heart is filling with blood, there is still pressure in the arteries because of the elastic rebound of the artery walls.

Blood pressure is measured in millimeters of mercury and is read in the form of a fraction, for example 120/80, in which the first number represents the **systolic pressure** when the heart is contracting, and the second is the **diastolic pressure** when the heart is at rest. The normal range of the systolic pressure in a healthy young adult at rest is 100 to 120. The diastolic pressure ranges from 60 to 80. Resting blood pressures above 140/90 are considered high blood pressure, which is called **hypertension**.

Unlike the heartbeat, which usually slows down as we get older, blood pressure rises with

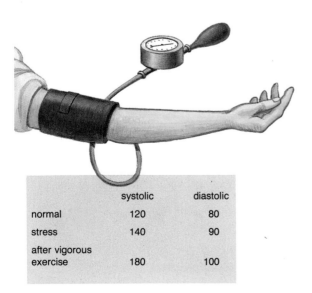

	systolic	diastolic
normal	120	80
stress	140	90
after vigorous exercise	180	100

age. A newborn baby has a systolic pressure of about 40 millimeters of mercury. By ten years it averages 100. At puberty the normal adult level is reached. By sixty years of age the average may be 140, and up to 160 by age eighty.

Blood pressure is measured using an instrument called a **sphygmomanometer** and a **stethoscope**. A cuff is wrapped around the arm just above the elbow and inflated with air to cut off the flow of blood to the lower arm. The air is slowly let out of the cuff while the doctor or nurse listens to the sounds coming from the artery with a stethoscope. The cuff is connected to a gauge that measures the air pressure in the cuff. When the blood pressure is higher than the pressure in the cuff, blood flows back into the artery during systole, and a tapping sound can be heard with the stethoscope. More air is let out of the cuff. When the sound fades away completely, the diastolic pressure is read on the dial.

Blood pressure depends on the amount of blood in the system, the rate and the strength of the heart's contractions, and how elastic the walls of the arteries are. It also varies according to what we're doing or how we're feeling. Exercise—even just rising from a sitting position to a standing one—can raise the blood pressure. Fear, excitement, worry, and other emotions can also increase blood pressure. Many people have higher-than-normal blood pressure readings in the doctor's office simply because they are nervous about getting their blood pressure taken. Depression, loneliness, and grief often cause blood pressure to drop.

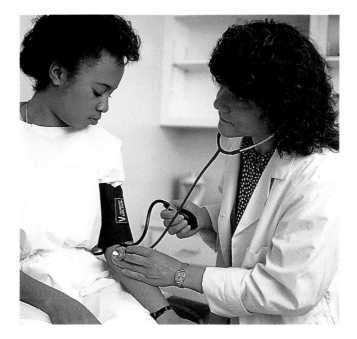

A blood pressure check is an important part of regular physical examinations.

A TRIP AROUND THE CIRCULATORY SYSTEM

Let's follow the path of a single drop of blood around the circulatory system as it makes its way through your body.

We'll start at your heart, the crossroads of the circulatory system. The heart's thick, muscular walls are relaxed. Our drop of bright red blood slips down into the left ventricle through the open mitral valve from the left atrium. But then, suddenly, the walls of the atrium squeeze in, sending more blood squirting in before the mitral valve slams shut. The walls of the ventricle heave in a mighty contraction, and the blood that fills it swirls around, then shoots upward, carrying the drop of blood we are following out through the aortic valve into the aorta.

The blood is a raging river now as it passes through the arteries. The channels get narrower, as the arteries branch again and again into smaller blood vessels. The many branches lead to all parts of the body.

The branch that we're following happens to lead to a fingertip on your right hand. Traveling across your shoulder and down your arm, the drop of blood passes into smaller arterioles and then into capillaries. It is moving slowly now (nearly a thousand times as slowly as in the aorta). The aorta was like a superhighway, but the capillaries are like side streets where the blood makes pickups and deliveries, bringing oxygen to the finger cells and picking up the cells' waste products. As the blood moves along, it darkens to a purplish color.

The capillary channel may be so narrow that the red blood cells floating along have to bend and squeeze to slip through. But then the channel gets wider as the capillary becomes a venule. The blood flows quietly on into a larger vein. As it makes its way up your arm, it must pass through a number of funnellike valves that keep it from slipping backward.

On the blood flows, through the widening channels of the veins, finally reaching the superior vena cava above the heart. Then the drop of blood plunges down into the cavelike chamber of your right atrium.

The walls of the cave seem to close down upon the blood in the atrium. The drop of blood shoots down, through the open tricuspid valve, with the stream that is squirting down into a larger and deeper cave. This is your right ventricle. The walls of the ventricle close in, and the blood is whisked upward through the pulmonary valve into the pulmonary artery. The blood is now on its way to the lungs.

Our drop of blood flows through a network of tiny capillaries in your left lung, very close to the surface of the many small air pockets. The walls of the capillaries are so thin that the waste products carried from the cells pass out of the blood to be exhaled in the lungs.

A well-functioning circulatory system allows us to enjoy many forms of exercise.

Oxygen that has been breathed into the lungs passes from the air pockets into the capillaries, and the blood picks up a load of oxygen.

The capillaries widen into veins. This trip is much shorter than the journey from the fingertip, and the blood enters the heart through a pulmonary vein. Our drop of blood plunges into the left atrium, where we started to follow its journey. The whole trip took less than a minute!

In later journeys our drop of blood may visit many other parts of the body, helping to carry digested food from the intestines, deliver wastes to the kidneys, or bring oxygen to the brain to help you think.

BLOOD

The common saying "blood is thicker than water" is really true. Blood is three to four times as thick as water. There is a lot of water in blood, but almost half its volume is made up of solid particles and cells.

When you look at a drop of blood it looks pretty uniform. But if you put the drop on a slide and look at it under a microscope, you can see flattened red doughnut-shaped disks floating lazily along. These disks are called **red blood cells**. They give blood its red color, and they carry oxygen and carbon dioxide around the body. You can also see colorless, irregularly shaped **white blood cells** creeping and oozing along the surface of the slide. They help defend the body against disease and infection. Smaller **platelets** are scattered about. They help the blood to thicken and **clot** when you get a cut. A single drop of blood contains more than 250 million blood cells! These cells are often called the **formed elements** because they have a form or shape. The formed elements make up about 45 percent of the total blood volume.

The solid part of the blood can be separated out using a machine called a centrifuge. A blood sample is placed in a test tube and spun at a high speed. The heavier parts of the blood sink to the bottom of the tube, and the lighter material remains at the top. The red mass at the bottom is red blood cells. Above it is a thin, whitish layer, which contains white blood cells and platelets. At the top of the tube is a clear, yellowish (straw-colored) liquid, called the blood **plasma**.

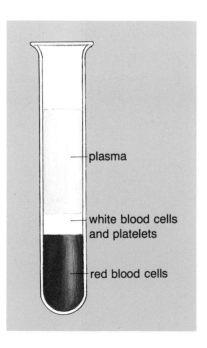

plasma

white blood cells and platelets

red blood cells

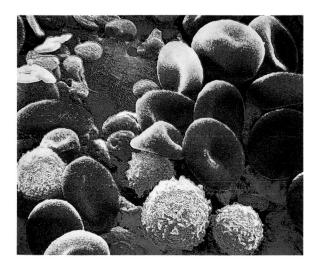

Blood cells photographed through a microscope

Plasma makes up 55 percent of the volume of the blood. The liquid part of blood provides a supply of water for the needs of the body cells. It helps distribute heat throughout the body to regulate our internal temperature. But plasma is not just water. Mixed in it are hundreds of kinds of chemicals such as proteins, salts, and various others. (Have you ever sucked on a cut finger? You can taste the saltiness of blood.) Blood carries a sugar called **glucose** to supply energy for the cells. Some proteins in the blood are enzymes that help other chemicals react. Some are hormones, which carry messages telling various body cells and organs what to do. Researchers have not yet been able to create an artificial substitute that performs all of the functions of blood.

The amount of blood in a person's body depends on how big the person is. If you weigh 100 pounds, you have about 7 pounds of blood. An average-sized adult man has about 5 to 7 quarts (4.8 to 6.6 liters) of blood flowing through his blood vessels—about 7 percent of the total weight of his body. Women have less blood than men, 4 to 6 quarts (3.8 to 5.7 liters) on the average. Volume also depends on age: babies have a greater proportion of blood compared to their body weight than adults.

Most cells in the body spend their whole lives in one place. But the formed elements of the blood are constantly on the move. In the capillaries, fluids and gases are continually being exchanged back and forth between the blood and the cells. Thus, the blood is ever changing. And yet, overall, its composition remains surprisingly constant.

BLOOD PLASMA

Plasma is what makes blood liquid. If the formed elements were not carried by plasma, the heart would not be able to move them around the body. The term *plasma* comes from a Greek word for "something that doesn't have any particular shape."

Blood plasma is 92 percent water. But the other 8 percent of the plasma includes thousands of different substances, dissolved in the water.

Proteins make up more than half the weight of substances in the plasma. Some of the thousands of plasma proteins help to control how much water enters and leaves the capillaries, keeping the amount of plasma in the blood vessels at the right level. Others help to maintain normal blood pressure. Some plasma proteins help to keep chemicals such as acids and bases in balance to make sure the environment is just right for the body cells. (Too much acid or base could poison body cells.) Special proteins called antibodies combine with "foreign" materials such as those found on invading germs or cells that have become cancerous. Another plasma protein, **fibrinogen**, is important in helping blood to clot. The liquid that remains after fibrinogen is removed from plasma is called serum.

Hormones are chemicals produced by endocrine glands to control many different activities in the body. Insulin, for example, is produced by the pancreas and helps the body to burn glucose, its main energy fuel. Growth hormone helps the body to grow, and sex hormones aid in the formation and work of the reproductive organs. Adrenaline speeds up the heartbeat during an emergency.

Glucose in the blood is used as an energy source by the body cells. After a meal the glucose level goes up, but the level quickly falls as the sugar is taken up by the cells. Extra plasma glucose is changed into a starch called glycogen and stored in the liver. When supplies get low, glycogen is changed back into glucose and supplied to the circulating blood as it is needed. Insulin and other hormones work to keep the amount of glucose in the blood at about the right level.

Lipids are fatty chemicals. The blood lipids include fats and cholesterol. Both are needed by the body, but high cholesterol levels in the blood could cause this lipid to be deposited in the artery walls. This can cause a narrowing of the blood vessels, which can lead to heart attacks or strokes.

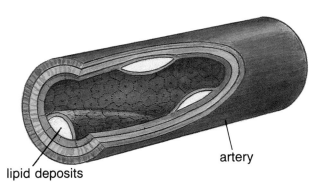

lipid deposits

artery

Too much cholesterol in the blood may cause deposits on artery walls, restricting blood flow.

Salts make up nearly 1 percent of the blood. That's why blood tastes salty. Salts are important in the work of the muscles and nerves, in building and maintaining bones and teeth, and in many other important uses. But too much salt can cause problems. Excess salt is removed by the kidneys.

Plasma carries waste products, such as urea, a chemical produced when proteins are broken down. Urea is delivered to the kidneys and sweat glands to be released. Another important cell waste product, carbon dioxide, is formed when cells use sugars or fats to produce energy. This waste product leaves the body mainly through the lungs.

Plasma helps to even out the temperature in the body. It keeps body tissues from overheating the way a car radiator keeps a car engine from overheating. When our muscles are working, they produce heat. This extra heat is carried by the plasma to the blood vessels near the skin, which are cooled by the air.

RED BLOOD CELLS

Red blood cells give blood its red color. Their technical name, **erythrocyte** (from Greek words meaning "red" and "cell"), emphasizes their color. But under a microscope, red blood cells look yellowish, not red. Each one contains a red pigment called **hemoglobin**, but it is only the huge masses of red cells that together give blood its rich red color. (There are about 25 trillion red blood cells circulating through an adult's body.)

Red blood cells are shaped like doughnuts with the centers only partly scooped out. Normally they are all the same size, and perfectly round. The

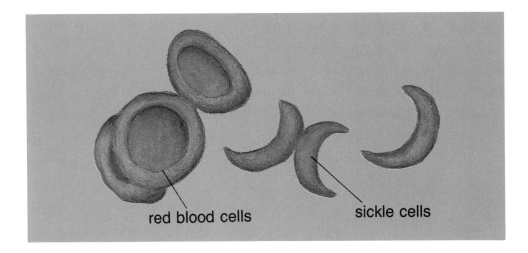

red blood cells   sickle cells

Normal red blood cells (left) are round and flow easily through blood vessels.
Abnormal cells (right) are called sickle cells. Their shape causes them to
clump together and become stuck in blood vessels.

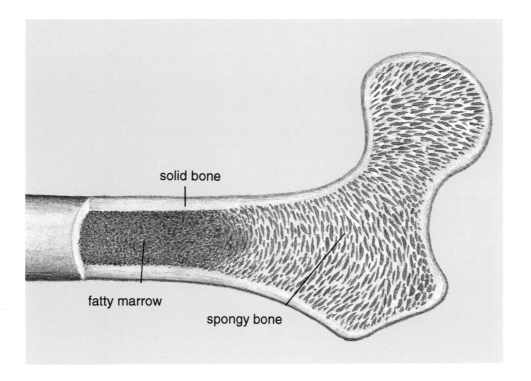

Red blood cells are produced in the spongy part of some bones.

red cells are small—about 0.0002 inch (7.5 micrometers) wide. Yet they are larger than the smallest capillaries, which are only 0.00013 inch (5 micrometers) wide—less than one-twentieth the width of a hair. Fortunately, these cells are soft and flexible, so they can bend and twist as they pass single file through the capillaries of the body. Red cells cannot move on their own but are carried in the flow of blood. Sometimes they pile up against one another like a stack of coins.

Misshapen red blood cells, called sickle cells, clump together and plug up blood vessels. This painful inherited condition is known as sickle-cell anemia.

Hemoglobin molecules make up one-third the weight of a red blood cell. They are proteins combined with a red chemical that contains iron. Oxygen can combine with the iron, changing hemoglobin into a form called **oxyhemoglobin**. Hemoglobin can pick up more than half its own

BLUE BLOODS

A "blue blood" is someone who is born into a noble family. The phrase comes from Spain. The Castilians of the north claimed they had blue blood because their veins were very visible beneath their fair skin. The southern Spaniards they ruled had darker complexions, so their veins were less visible.

Some animals are *really* blue-blooded. A lobster's blood, for example, does not contain hemoglobin. Instead, oxygen is carried by a bright blue pigment called hemocyanin.

WHY A BRUISE TURNS BLACK AND BLUE

When you get a cut, blood from a broken blood vessel flows out of the body. But in a bruise a blood vessel under the skin is broken. Red blood cells that leak out into the tissues lose their oxygen, and the hemoglobin turns a bluish purple color. Later, as hemoglobin is broken down, the bruise may turn yellowish or greenish.

weight in oxygen. Normally it is a purplish color, but when it is carrying oxygen it turns a bright red.

Hemoglobin can also combine with carbon dioxide. Both oxygen and carbon dioxide are only loosely attached to hemoglobin so that they are easily transferred. But hemoglobin can bind tightly to carbon monoxide, a poisonous gas present in the fumes from leaking furnaces and automobile exhausts. A person can die from breathing carbon monoxide because it ties up hemoglobin molecules so that they can't carry oxygen to the body cells.

Red blood cells are unusual. Unlike all other body cells, they do not have a nucleus, a major control center that directs and coordinates the cell's activities.

Red blood cells are produced in the bone marrow, the spongy part inside some of the bones. Their parent cells do have a nucleus, but it is lost as the red cell is formed.

A working red blood cell lives for only about 120 days. Worn-out cells are taken out of circulation in the spleen and liver. Some of the iron from their hemoglobin is sent to the bone marrow to be reused, but some is excreted. (That is why we need to take in new supplies of iron in the food we eat.) The liver can change the hemoglobin pigment into green bile, which helps digest fats.

WHITE BLOOD CELLS

The body has many defenses against disease germs. The skin is like a protective wall around us. Mucous membranes line the entrances into the body to catch intruders in sticky mucus. Stomach acids kill bacteria that are swallowed. When bacteria or viruses get into the body, though, white blood cells are like soldiers that attack and destroy these invaders.

White blood cells are called **leukocytes**, which means "white cells." Like the red blood cells, they have a rather misleading name: white blood cells are actually not white; they are colorless, jellylike blobs.

White blood cells are larger than red blood cells, but there are far fewer of them. There is only one white cell for every 700 red cells. (A normal person has 5,000 to 10,000 white blood cells in a cubic microliter of blood.) The white cells make up 10 percent of the total volume of blood.

White blood cells can move on their own. They use the bloodstream the way a commuter uses a highway to drive to work. They can even travel against the current. The white cells move by changing their shape. Their bodies ooze along by sending out armlike pseudopods (literally, "false feet"). A portion of the cell bulges out into a pseudopod, and the cell contents flow into it.

A white cell can even leave the bloodstream, by squeezing through the walls of capillaries into the surrounding tissue, where bacteria have caused infection. White blood cells also change shape to swallow up invaders. Their soft body wraps around an invader until it is trapped inside. Then digestive chemicals break down the germ.

There are five kinds of white blood cells, which make up two main families.

white blood cells

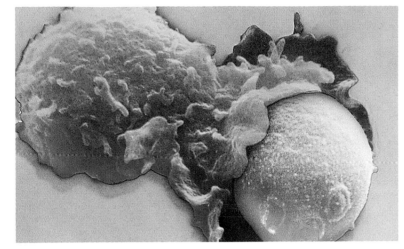

A lymphocyte engulfing a yeast cell

The **granulocytes**, which contain tiny grains, make up about 65 percent of all the white blood cells and include the **eosinophils, basophils,** and **neutrophils**. The white blood cells of the other family, the **lymphocytes** and **monocytes**, do not have a grainy texture. Granulocytes and monocytes are produced in the bone marrow. Lymphocytes come from the **lymph nodes**, the spleen, the thymus, the tonsils, and other parts of the lymph system.

Neutrophils are the most numerous white blood cells, more than 60 percent of the total. They are the first onto the battlefield. Neutrophils gobble up bacteria and other invaders. But bacteria contain poisons. After a neutrophil has eaten between five and twenty-five bacteria, it dies. Pus, a thick, yellowish liquid that may form after an infection, is made up mostly of dead neutrophils, along with bits of cell debris.

Eosinophils make up only about 2 percent of the leukocytes. They contain special enzymes that detoxify foreign substances so they can't hurt the body. Eosinophils help to fight parasites and combat allergic reactions.

Basophils are the rarest of the white blood cells. They release chemicals that help in the process of inflammation and healing.

About 30 percent of the white blood cells are lymphocytes. They battle germs and other "foreign" invaders. Lymphocytes can travel back and forth from blood to tissue, into lymph nodes and back into the blood.

Monocytes are the largest white blood cells. They make up about 5 percent of the total. After a few hours in the tissue, monocytes swell to become **macrophages** (which literally means "big eaters"). One macrophage can eat up to 100 bacteria, as well as large particles of cell fragments or foreign matter.

THE IMMUNE SYSTEM

Many of the uncomfortable symptoms of an illness are actually side effects of the body's fight against the invading germs. The damaged cells release chemical alarm signals that produce **inflammation**: redness, swelling, pain, and a hot feeling. Blood vessels become enlarged, bringing large amounts of fresh blood to the area. Water from blood plasma seeps into the surrounding tissues, causing swelling. Blood brings white blood cells into the tissue. They start killing bacteria and cleaning up debris. They also release chemicals that call more white blood cells into the area.

Every germ that enters the body has its own pattern of chemicals on its outer surface, which are called **antigens**. Some lymphocytes produce antibodies that match up with specific antigens. The antibodies either break the germ apart or make the germs clump together so that the white blood cells can more easily destroy them.

Eventually the white blood cells get the infection under control. Some lymphocytes remember how to make the antibodies that attack that particular germ. Then, the next time germs of the same type get into the body, the immune system will be able to quickly kill them off before the disease can develop. This is called **immunity.**

You don't have to get a disease to become immune to it, though. **Vaccinations** can immunize us against many diseases. A solution of weak or dead germs is used to trick the body into producing antibodies against the germ. Then, if the real disease germs get into the body, we will be immune to them. Immunizations are given against measles, mumps, rubella, tetanus, polio, diphtheria, and whooping cough. Some are injected into the body and some are taken by mouth. It is hard to immunize the body against some germs, such as influenza and the common cold, because the

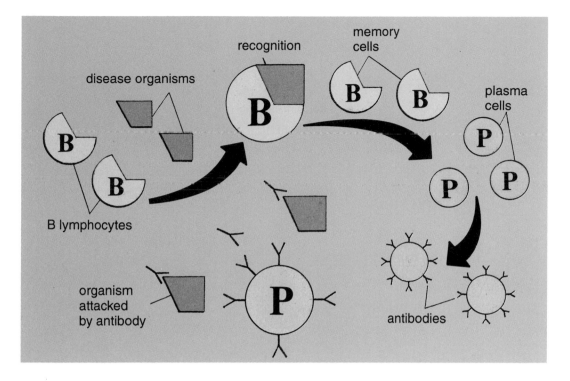

When B cells recognize a particular disease organism, they multiply rapidly into plasma cells. The plasma cells make antibodies to attack the disease organism. After infection, some B memory cells develop and will be the ones to quickly make antibodies if the same disease organism strikes again.

virus is always changing its outer surface just enough so that the body can't recognize it.

Doctors may give injections to provide temporary immunity. **Gamma globulin** (antibodies against disease germs) and **antitoxins** (antibodies against bacterial poisons) can prevent illness after people have been exposed to germs causing diseases such as measles, hepatitis, and tetanus.

There are two types of lymphocytes, **B cells** and **T cells**. B cells make antibodies. T cells kill invaders and also control immune processes. They also check body cells for "foreign" chemicals and kill any that have become cancerous. Unfortunately, when a person receives a transplanted organ, the lymphocytes think it is foreign and attack it. When transplants are per-

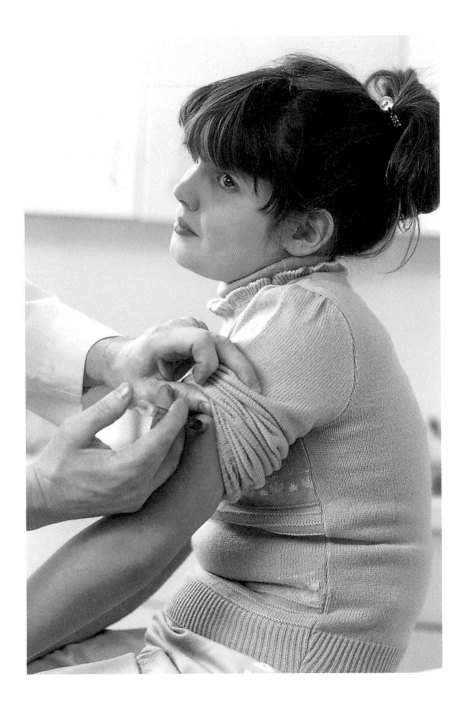

A young patient gets a booster for diphtheria, tetanus, and whooping cough. The vaccine is usually given first in several stages between two months and fifteen months of age.

formed, special drugs are used to suppress this immune response, but this lowers the body's defenses against infections and cancer.

During an infection the number of white blood cells can increase greatly. Different types of infections cause an increase in different white blood cells. By examining blood samples, doctors can get a better idea of the type of infection going on in a person's body.

Sometimes the immune system doesn't work properly. **Allergies** are caused by the body's reactions to foreign substances like plant pollens, which are not really harmful. Sometimes the body's immune system mistakes its own healthy cells for foreign ones and begins to attack them. This reaction is called an **autoimmune response**. Doctors believe that many diseases, including multiple sclerosis and rheumatoid arthritis, are autoimmune diseases.

SECTION 3

BLOOD CLOTTING

When a blood vessel is cut, blood spills out of it. Very heavy bleeding is referred to as a **hemorrhage**. The loss of blood means that there is less circulating in the blood vessels. The blood pressure drops, and if too much blood is lost, the person can go into shock and the heart might stop beating. Losing about two pints of blood can lead to death.

Fortunately, the body has an effective safety mechanism to limit blood loss. When blood is exposed to air, it forms a kind of semisolid gel. This is called **coagulation** or blood clotting. The clot acts as a plug, preventing further loss of blood from the cut vessel. If blood didn't clot, we could bleed to death from even the simplest scratch.

Blood platelets are a key link in the clotting process. Platelets are much smaller than the tiny red blood cells. (Red blood cells are eight times as heavy and twice as wide.) There are 250,000 to 400,000 platelets per cubic millimeter of blood—more than white blood cells but less than red blood

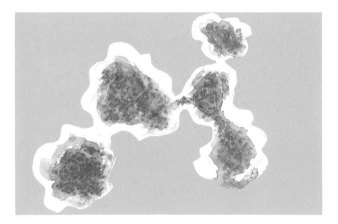

Platelets clump together to form a plug when a blood vessel is cut.

cells. The drop of blood that oozes out when you prick your finger contains about 15 million platelets. Platelets got their name because under a microscope they look like little oval plates. They are also called **thrombocytes**, which means "clotting cells." However, they are not really cells, but only fragments of cells without a nucleus.

Platelets are formed in

the bone marrow. They live for about a week, if they aren't needed sooner. A blood platelet can perform its special service for the body only once, for it is destroyed in the act.

When a blood vessel is cut, the damaged edges are rough. Within seconds, platelets stick to the roughened edges. The platelets swell and secrete a substance that attracts other platelets. They begin to clump together, forming a plug. If the hole is small enough, the platelet plug can close it entirely. Hundreds of tiny tears in our capillaries may be fixed this way each day.

If the hole is too large or the vessel is cut through, the platelets help out further. They are very delicate, and when exposed to air or rough surfaces they break open, spilling out many different substances. Some chemicals cause the blood vessels to become narrower, cutting down the supply of blood so that less will leak out. A substance called **platelet factor** begins a chain of chemical reactions that turns a blood plasma protein, fibrinogen, into **fibrin**—long, yellow, sticky fibers. The fibers tangle together, creating a cobweblike mesh. Platelets and red and white blood cells are caught up in the crisscrossing protein fibers and form a thickened lump called a clot, which plugs up the hole. Once the clot has formed, the fibers shrink, squeezing out most of the fluid. The clot is changed from a soft mass into a firm one, which helps even more to stop bleeding.

A blood clot provides the framework for new tissue to be built. New skin cells, connective tissue, and new capillaries fill in the wound. If the cut is on the skin, the hardened blood forms a scab, which helps to keep germs out of the body while regrowth and repair work go on beneath it.

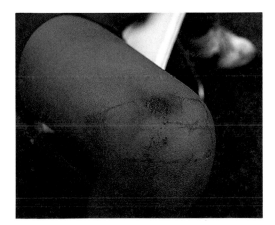

Clotting is a fairly complicated process, involving at least a dozen chemical reactions. It's a good thing it can't happen too easily, or blood might clot inside the blood vessels and block them.

A scab forms a protective coating over a wound while healing takes place beneath.

BLOOD TYPES AND BLOOD TRANSFUSIONS

The ancient Incas in South America used blood transfusions. When someone had lost a lot of blood, blood from a donor was placed in the patient's veins. In many cases this saved the person's life. In the 1600s, European doctors tried to replace lost blood, too. Sometimes it worked, but often the person died. Many countries outlawed blood transfusions.

No one knew why transfusions weren't always effective until 1901. Karl Landsteiner, an Austrian doctor, discovered that red blood cells contain antigens or agglutinogens on their surface that can react with antibodies (agglutinins) in the plasma of some other people's blood. Normally, a person's blood does not contain the antibodies that attack the antigens on his or her own red cells. But when blood samples that don't match are mixed, antibodies attack the antigens, and the red cells clump together (agglutinate). It was this **agglutination** reaction that was killing the early transfusion patients.

Landsteiner found there were four main blood types: A, B, AB, and O. A person with type O blood has no antigens on the red blood cells, but has *a* and *b* antibodies in the plasma. People with this type are **universal donors** because they can give blood to people with any blood type without danger of agglutination. A person with type A blood has *A* antigens on the red blood cells, and *b* antibodies in the plasma. A person with type B blood has *B* antigens and *a* antibodies. A person with type AB blood has *A* and *B* antigens, but no antibodies. People with type AB blood are universal recipients because they can safely receive blood of any blood type.

Landsteiner won a Nobel prize for discovering the ABO system. He also found other differences in blood, such as M and N factors and **Rh factor** (named for the rhesus monkeys in which it was first found). Each set

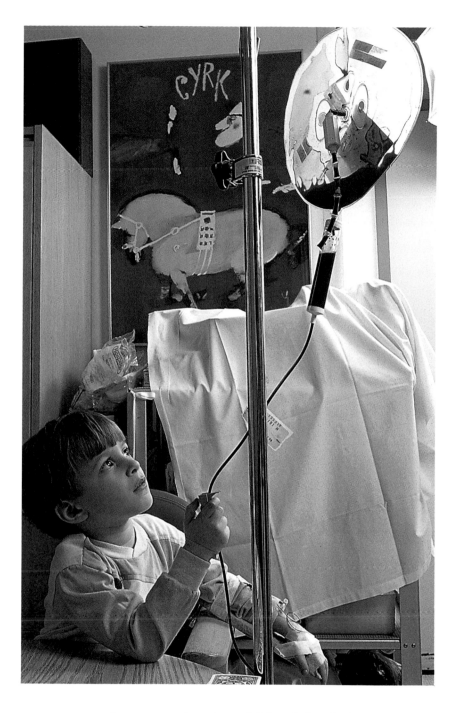

*A young patient in a children's hospital
receives blood from a blood bank.*

of blood group factors is inherited independently, giving a person a characteristic "blood type."

Quick blood tests were developed to determine blood types so that people could be given blood of the right type when a transfusion was needed. In early blood transfusions, blood was allowed to flow from the donor's vein through a needle and tubing into the recipient's vein. Today, donor blood is collected and stored in blood banks until it is needed. Millions of pints of blood are donated and used every year. Because diseases can be spread through donated blood, before blood is accepted from donors it is tested for diseases such as hepatitis, syphilis, and AIDS.

Blood can be stored at cold temperatures for up to three weeks before red cells begin to break down. Scientists have found many other ways to

Donated blood can be stored in sterile plastic bags
at cold temperatures for up to three weeks.

make blood last longer. In some emergency situations, such as on the battlefront or in an ambulance at the scene of an accident, plasma or even salt or sugar solutions can help to restore lost blood volume until the oxygen-carrying red blood cells can be replaced. Researchers are also working to perfect completely synthetic blood substitutes.

The Rh factor doesn't usually cause problems in transfusions, but it can be important if an Rh negative woman is pregnant with an Rh positive baby. Leaks in the **placenta** may allow her blood and the baby's to mix. Then she may begin producing Rh antibodies that could attack the baby's blood cells. The RhoGAM vaccine is now used to prevent such problems. It is given to an Rh negative woman several weeks before she gives birth and is administered again within 24 hours after birth. The vaccine contains Rh antibodies, which signal to the woman's immune system that she is already protected against the antigen. No new antibodies are produced, and the ones that were injected break down and disappear before they have a chance to harm a subsequent baby.

THE LYMPH SYSTEM

In addition to the two "red rivers" of the body, the pulmonary and systemic circulatory systems, there is a third circulatory system—the "white river" of the **lymphatic system**.

The vessels of the lymphatic system are very much like the veins and capillaries of the blood system. Lymph vessels are found all over the body, wherever there are blood vessels, and the lymphatic system works closely with the circulatory system.

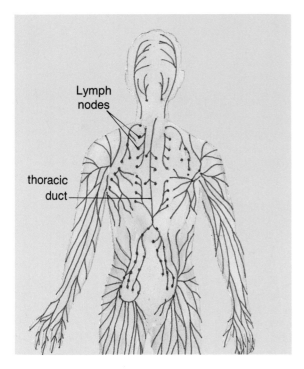

The lymphatic system is an extensive drainage system designed to handle fluid that bathes body tissues.

The walls of the blood capillaries are very thin and have many tiny openings. Gases and chemicals can pass in and out, feeding the cells and taking away their waste products. But the openings also allow fluid from the blood to leak out. This fluid flows out of the capillaries and bathes the body tissues. If there were no way to drain it, fluid would build up in the tissues until our bodies swelled up like balloons.

Lymph vessels recycle the fluid, returning it to the circulatory system. This clear, watery fluid drains into open-ended, one-way lymph capillaries. Now called **lymph**, it contains nutrients, waste products, white blood cells, proteins, and other chemicals. From the capillaries it flows along larger and larger veinlike channels, called **lymphatics**, into two main lymph vessels near the base of the neck. The **thoracic duct** is the main trunk of the lymphatic system. It enters a large vein close to the heart on the left. The **lymphatic duct** enters a vein on the right side.

The lymphatic system is also important in transporting nutrients and wastes. Some molecules are too big to pass from the tissues into the capillaries of the circulatory system. Proteins manufactured by body tissues, for example, are carried in the lymphatic system. Lymph carries fats from the walls of the small intestine to the liver.

Lymph does not have a pump like the heart to move it along through vessels in the body. The movements of muscles and the rhythmic contraction of the arteries squeeze the lymph vessels, pushing lymph along. The constant pressure of new fluid in the tissues helps to keep lymph flowing. Like veins, large lymphatic vessels have valves to prevent backflow.

Scattered throughout the lymphatic system are a number of swellings, called lymph nodes. They are grouped in large numbers in some areas of the body, such as in the neck, under the jaw, in the groin area, in the armpits, and near the liver and small intestines. Lymph nodes contain filters to remove and destroy germs and poisons. Lymphocytes are also made in the lymph nodes to help fight diseases.

You may have noticed that sometimes when you are sick, painful lumps may develop on the sides of your neck, in your armpits, and in other parts of your body. These are swollen lymph nodes, indicating that these glands are fighting disease germs. The tonsils contain lymphatic tissue and also may become enlarged when your body is battling an infection.

The spleen is a spongy mass of lymphoid tissue that filters out germs and also produces white blood cells. This bean-shaped organ, about the size of your heart, is found on the left side of the stomach. Unlike other lymphoid tissue, the spleen contains red blood cells. It squeezes in and out, helping to control the amount of blood and blood cells flowing through the body. Old, worn-out red blood cells are broken apart in the spleen.

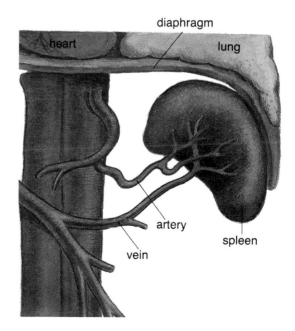

THE KIDNEYS

The kidneys are not really a part of the circulatory system, but they play an important role in its work. These two bean-shaped organs, each the size of a child's fist, are located one on each side, just above the waistline in the back of the abdomen. Together the kidneys weigh less than a pound, but they receive more than 20 percent of the blood flow from the heart.

Renal arteries bring blood into the kidneys. Each artery divides into smaller and smaller branches. Each branch ends in a microscopic filter called a nephron, where harmful substances are removed from the blood and sent out of the body, while useful substances are carefully saved and returned to the blood. There are more than 2 million nephrons in your kidneys. They cleanse all the blood in your body every 50 minutes.

The arterioles that lead into the nephron form a tangled knot of capillaries called a **glomerulus**. That is the first part of the filter. Water with dissolved salts and other chemicals passes out through the thin capillary walls and is funneled into a collecting tube. Blood cells and proteins stay behind in the capillaries. These tiny filters remove about 50 gallons (190 liters) of fluid from the blood each day. Imagine how much water you'd have to drink to replace all that fluid (and how many times you'd have to go to the bathroom)! Fortunately, that's just the beginning of the story. You'd expect the capillaries of the glomerulus to lead to venules. But instead, they drain into more arterioles. Those lead to a network of capillaries surrounding the looping collecting tube in which urine is forming. In that part of the nephron, a lot of the water is returned to the blood, along with things the body can use, such as glucose and salts. The kidneys work to keep the water, salts, and other chemicals in the blood in just the right proportions.

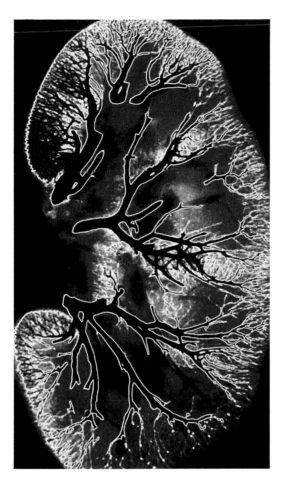

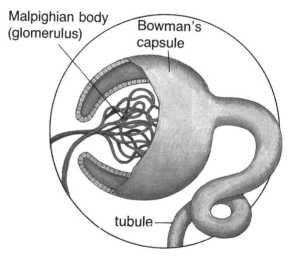

◀ A color enhanced photo of a kidney showing the vast network of blood vessels that keep it functioning

Malpighian body
(glomerulus)

Bowman's
capsule

tubule

▶ A glomerulus is a tangle of capillaries that make up the first part of a kidney's filtering system.

Meanwhile, harmful waste products stay in the collecting tube and are sent to the bladder with the urine. One of the main waste products excreted by the kidneys is urea, which is formed when proteins are broken down. If it were allowed to accumulate in the blood, it could poison body cells. When your bladder feels full, you urinate and get rid of the urea and other wastes.

kidney

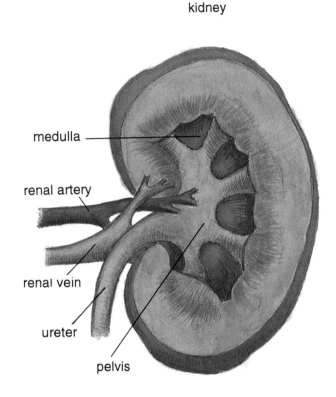

medulla

renal artery

renal vein

ureter

pelvis

This cross section of a kidney shows its major parts.

Blood pressure helps to make the kidney filters work, and the kidneys themselves help to regulate blood pressure. They do this by constantly adjusting the amount of blood circulating through the body. The kidneys also produce a chemical called **renin**, which helps to form a blood-pressure-raising hormone (**angiotensin**) when the pressure in the arteries is too low.

The kidneys also help to determine how many new red blood cells are created. If the blood flowing through the kidneys is low in oxygen, the kidneys produce a hormone called **erythropoietin**, which increases the production of red cells. This hormone helps to form more red blood cells when people move to mountain areas. At high altitudes there is less oxygen, so the body needs more red blood cells to deliver the oxygen that is available to the body cells.

DID YOU KNOW . . .

The heart produces a hormone that helps to regulate the kidneys. Atrial natriuretic factor increases the excretion of salt in the urine and helps to lower blood pressure.

AMAZING CHANGES

From the time when you were just a mass of cells no bigger than a pinhead, you were connected to your mother's womb by the ropelike **umbilical cord**. A network of tiny tubes formed and began to carry oxygen and food materials from your mother's blood. There was no direct connection between her bloodstream and yours. An exchange of gases very much like the one that goes on in your lungs now took place in a structure called the placenta, on the inner surface of the womb.

By the end of your third week, two small tubes, surrounded by a coat of muscle cells, began to join. In just a day or two, the tubes were joined into a single-chambered heart that was smaller than the period at the end of this sentence. The heart was the first organ in your body to be formed, and it was the first to start working. About twenty-two days after you started out as a single cell, when you were just about 0.06 inch (1.5 millimeters) long, your heart began to beat, pumping blood through your tiny body.

In the weeks that followed, you grew and took shape, and so did your heart. Soon it had two chambers, an atrium and a ventricle, and it was twisted first into an S shape and later into a U shape. During your fifth week, the atrium divided, forming two separate pathways for blood. (A small opening between the two atria, called the **foramen ovale**, still remained, though, permitting a little mixing of the blood flows.) Later the septum grew down the middle of the ventricle to form the left and right pumping chambers. By the end of your eighth week, when you were about 1 inch (2.5 centimeters) long, your heart was a tiny copy of an adult heart.

Through all the rest of your time before birth, your heart continued to beat. Your blood carried oxygen and nutrients to your body cells and took away their waste products. But the gas exchange still took place at the placenta. Your lungs were filled with fluid, and they had never been used. They received only enough blood to help them grow; most of the blood pumped into the pulmonary artery was drained off through a small connecting vessel into the aorta.

Then came your birth, when you were suddenly pushed out of your warm, watery, womb-world. You took your first breath and filled your lungs with air. That was a big change, and your circulatory system had to make some major changes, too. The blood vessels in your umbilical cord were clamped shut, cutting off the flow of blood to and from the placenta. The small blood vessel that had connected the pulmonary artery and aorta closed also, and so did the foramen ovale between the two atria. Now your blood began to travel through the two main loops of the circulatory system, the pulmonary and systemic systems. Within a week or so, the stump of your umbilical cord shriveled up and dropped off, leaving your belly button to mark the place where it was attached.

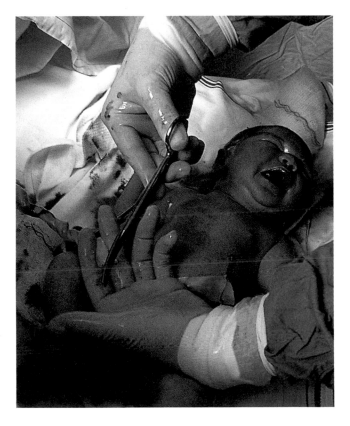

A doctor cuts the umbilical cord of a newborn, severing the connection to the placenta.

BLOOD DISORDERS

Many things can go wrong with blood. For example, some people are very pale and are tired all the time. They may be suffering from **anemia**, which means "lack of blood." Actually, something is wrong with the red blood cells, and not enough oxygen is being delivered to the body cells.

The most common form of anemia is iron-deficiency anemia. It occurs when the diet does not provide enough iron to form hemoglobin for new red blood cells. A lack of vitamin B_{12} and folic acid can also cause anemia because these vitamins help in the formation of red blood cells. Aplastic anemia can result when radiation or chemicals damage the bone marrow, preventing it from producing enough red blood cells. The number of red blood cells is also reduced when a lot of blood has been lost, in an accident or by internal bleeding, for example, from stomach ulcers.

Some hereditary conditions result in red blood cells that are not able to carry enough oxygen, or that tear open easily. **Sickle-cell anemia**, which occurs mainly among people of African descent, is one of the most common. A tiny change in hemoglobin results in misshapen red blood cells that can clump and plug up blood vessels, or rupture, causing anemia. **Cooley's anemia** is a similar condition in people of Mediterranean descent.

Blood clotting is a very complicated process, in which many things can go wrong. The liver produces many of the clotting factors, so liver damage can cause problems in blood clotting. Nutrition is also very important. A lack of vitamin K, which helps in the formation of a key clotting factor, can lead to faulty blood clotting. Damage to the bone marrow by drugs or radiation can reduce the number of platelets.

Some people inherit a disease called **hemophilia** and are unable to produce one or more of the blood-clotting factors. Even a small cut could result in bleeding to death. The most famous cases of hemophilia occurred when Queen Victoria passed the gene down to her children and grandchildren and spread the disease to several European royal families. Hemophiliacs today can lead almost normal lives by injecting themselves with the clotting factors that they are missing.

Leukemia is a form of cancer in which white blood cell production goes out of control in the bone marrow. *Leukemia* means "white blood," and fifty to sixty times the usual number of white blood cells (many of them abnormal) may be produced. Anemia develops because the white blood cells crowd out the developing red blood cells. The white blood cells plug up key blood vessels in the brain, heart, lungs, and kidneys and interfere with the functioning of bones, lymph nodes, spleen, liver, and other organs. Bone marrow transplants may help prolong the person's life.

Infectious mononucleosis is caused by the Epstein-Barr virus. The symptoms of this disease, which occurs most often in adolescents and young adults, are fever, sore throat, swollen lymph nodes, and extreme tiredness. Mono causes an increase in white blood cells that are larger than normal. Unlike leukemia, the body can get the disease under control on its own after a few weeks of battling the infected white blood cells.

In **AIDS**, a virus called HIV attacks the T lymphocytes that help B cells make antibodies. People with AIDS are unable to fight off infections that a normal immune system could handle easily.

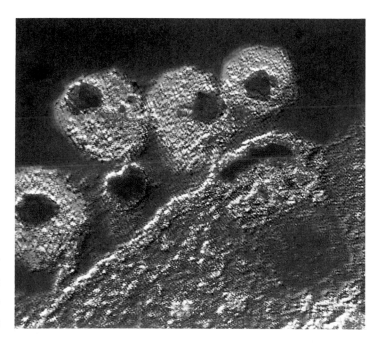

AIDS viruses emerging from a T4 lymphocyte that served as a host to the viruses

VASCULAR PROBLEMS

Vascular problems (those affecting blood vessels) can be mild or very serious. **Varicose veins**, for example, are fairly common and usually more of a nuisance than a threat to life. The problem typically occurs in the lower legs. When the valves in the veins do not work properly, blood may seep back down, pooling in the legs. The veins stand out and may swell to four times their normal size. People who stand a lot and women who have had many children have a greater chance of suffering from varicose veins. Treatment may include surgery or simply wearing support hosiery and keeping the feet up as much as possible. Overstretched veins can also develop in the wall of the rectum. Varicose veins occurring in this area are called **hemorrhoids**. They may bleed and can be very painful.

Varicose veins can lead to **phlebitis**, an inflammation of a vein, often in the leg. It may occur after long periods of bed rest. This is a serious condition because it can lead to a clot called a **thrombus** in the vein. The clot may break loose from the wall of the vein (then it is called an **embolus**) and travel through the bloodstream. If it becomes stuck in a pulmonary artery, it can stop the flow of blood to part of the lungs.

Hypertension doesn't mean being very tense; it is the medical term for high blood pressure, which persists even when the person is resting. Many people do not know they have high blood pressure, because often there are no symptoms. But hypertension can cause serious problems—stroke, heart disease, blood vessel damage, and damage to the eyes and kidneys. Smoking and eating too much salt can make hypertension worse. People with hypertension may be able to bring their blood pressure under control by watching what they eat, losing excess weight, exercising more, or taking special medications.

Arteriosclerosis, or hardening of the arteries, starts with a buildup of fatty deposits in the lining of the arteries. Scientists believe that a diet high in fat and cholesterol may help to cause this buildup. When minerals are added, the deposits become harder and begin to block the blood flow. The narrowing of the artery also makes it easier for blood clots to form.

A **stroke** occurs when the blood supply to a part of the brain is cut off, and the brain cells don't get the oxygen they need. This may happen when an artery leading to the brain is blocked by arteriosclerosis, a blood clot, or an air bubble. It can also occur when a blood vessel in the brain ruptures and bleeds into the brain tissue. (A weak spot in a blood vessel, which may bulge out like a balloon and finally burst, is called an **aneurysm**.) If the blockage is only temporary, the effects (such as slurred speech and weakness in the hands or feet) may disappear in a few hours. But severe strokes cause brain cells to die and may result in permanent paralysis on one or both sides of the body. If the stroke affects the part of the brain that controls an important body function, such as respiration, the person may die. Stroke is the third leading cause of death in the United States.

Gangrene means "dead flesh"; it occurs when circulation to a part of the body is cut off, and the cells die and begin to decay. Severe frostbite, for example, may destroy blood vessels in the hands or feet. Infections, severe burns, injuries that crush blood vessels, and uncontrolled diabetes can also lead to gangrene.

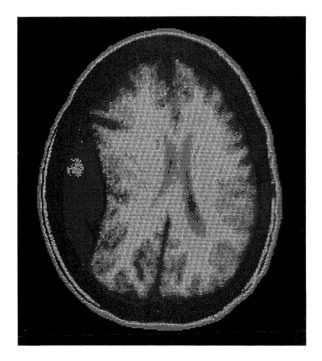

This brain scan shows a recent hemorrhage (the red oval area at far left).

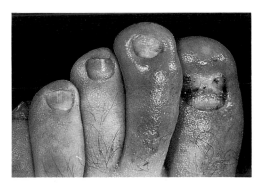

Severe frostbite injury

HEART PROBLEMS

Cardiovascular diseases (those affecting the heart and blood vessels) are the leading cause of death in the United States and the other industrialized nations. We tend to think of them as diseases of older people because most cardiovascular problems develop over a long time. But some can affect young people, too.

Some babies are born with hearts that don't function properly. Such conditions, already present at birth, are referred to as congenital. Congenital heart defects may be inherited, or they may be the result of something that happened while the baby was developing inside the mother. Cigarettes, alcohol, drugs, and infections such as German measles (rubella) can affect a developing fetus. The most common congenital heart problem is a hole in the wall that separates the two sides of the heart. Babies with this problem are often called "blue babies" because deoxygenated blood mixes with oxygenated blood, giving their skin a bluish color. Doctors can repair this and other heart defects surgically.

The hearts of children and adolescents may become damaged after a strep throat infection that leads to **rheumatic fever**. Rheumatic fever can thicken and scar the heart valves, so blood does not flow properly through the heart and it has to work harder. Rheumatic heart disease can be prevented by testing for strep whenever a child has a bad sore throat and treating the infections with antibiotics.

Bacterial infections can cause other heart problems, as well. In **endocarditis** the lining of the chambers of the heart and the valves becomes inflamed and covered with wartlike growths. **Myocarditis** is an inflammation of the heart muscle. **Pericarditis** is an inflammation of the pericardium (the sac that surrounds the heart).

Coronary artery disease develops when one of the coronary arteries becomes blocked, usually as a result of arteriosclerosis. Then the heart cannot get the oxygen it needs to pump blood around the body. A pain in the chest called **angina pectoris** is a warning sign that the heart is not getting enough oxygen to keep up with the demands placed on it. If the artery becomes completely blocked, part of the heart may die. This is called a **myocardial infarction**, or a heart attack.

Sometimes things go wrong with the heart's electrical system. Impulses telling the heart muscles to contract together may not travel properly through the heart. This can cause **arrhythmias**, in which the heart beats abnormally. Some arrhythmias are nothing to worry about, but an arrhythmia in the ventricle, called **ventricular fibrillation**, is very serious. The heart quivers rapidly instead of contracting together as a single unit, and blood is not pumped around the body. Unless the normal rhythm is restored in a few minutes, **cardiac arrest** occurs—the heart stops. There is no heartbeat, no pulse, and no blood pressure. Medical personnel may give the person an electric shock with a defibrillator to get the heart back into the right rhythm. But heart cells die after ten minutes without oxygen, so an ambulance may arrive too late. Someone who knows how to do **CPR (cardiopulmonary resuscitation)** may be able to save the person's life. CPR is a combination of mouth-to-mouth breathing (to supply oxygen to the lungs) and pressing on the chest (to circulate the blood).

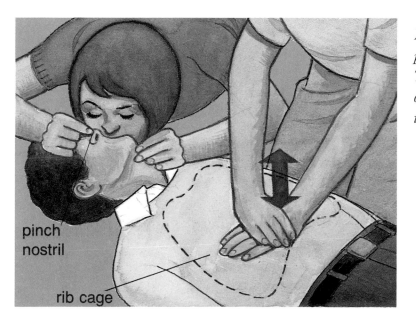

pinch
nostril

rib cage

Here, two trained people perform CPR on a victim. The Red Cross and other organizations offer courses to train people in CPR.

SEEING A DOCTOR

Simple tests of the heart and blood vessels are part of the usual routine each time you go to the doctor. The doctor or nurse checks your blood pressure and pulse rate, and the doctor listens to your heartbeat with a stethoscope. If any of the results seem suspicious, you may be sent to the hospital or to a heart specialist, called a **cardiologist**.

The cardiologist may run tests on blood and urine samples to find out if the organs of the body are functioning properly. When something is wrong with the circulatory system it affects the health of the rest of the body, too.

One of the most important tools for checking on the health of the heart is the **electrocardiograph**, or **EKG**. By recording the electrical activity of the heart, an EKG can show the doctor if heart muscle is injured or

electrocardiograph

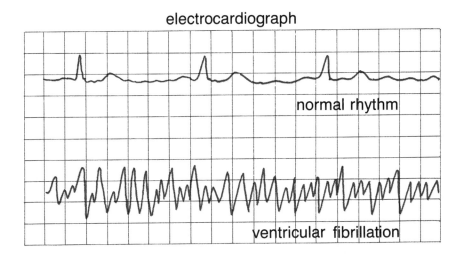

normal rhythm

ventricular fibrillation

overworked. An ordinary EKG is given while the patient is relaxed. But sometimes heart problems don't show up until the heart is pumping hard. In a **stress EKG** test the patient may walk on a treadmill or pedal a stationary bike while the EKG records the heart's activity. The doctor can also look for abnormalities that take place over a whole day of normal activity by hooking up a tiny, lightweight ambulatory EKG, which the patient wears throughout the day. The cardiologist can look over an entire day's heart activity in a few minutes.

A chest X ray can show whether the heart chambers are enlarged. (A failing heart may get larger as it vainly tries to pump enough blood.) To get a clearer picture of the heart, a cardiac catheter may be placed in a vein in the patient's arm. The thin plastic tube is slowly pushed along the bloodstream until it reaches the heart. The doctor can measure the blood pressure in the heart chambers, and can find out whether the blood in the

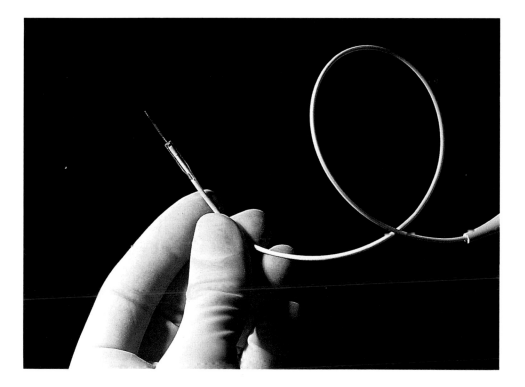

An optical fiber in a cardiac catheter can guide an
argon laser to vaporize deposits that clog coronary arteries.

chambers has a normal amount of oxygen. By injecting a dye through the catheter, the doctor can take X rays called **angiograms** that show how the dye moves through the blood vessels and heart chambers. The angiograms give a clear picture of valve leaks, damage, and inflammation in the heart.

The doctor can also look at blood vessels using a procedure called arteriography or angiography. Special dyes are injected into a patient's bloodstream. The dye shows up in X rays, and a computer helps put together an accurate picture of the blood vessels or the beating of the heart and shows it on a screen. The doctor can see many problems such as a coronary artery with arteriosclerosis that might cause a heart attack.

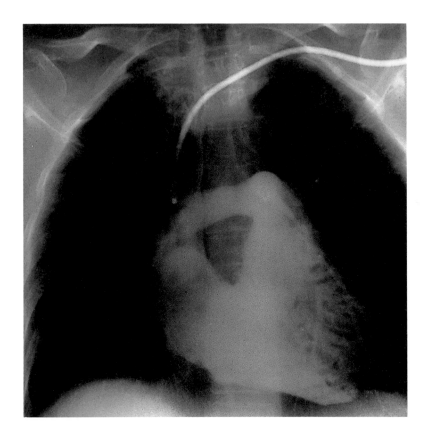

This angiogram shows a normal heart (pink). A dye was injected through a catheter into the right atrium to outline the right side of the heart. The blue areas are the diaphragm, ribs, and bones of the upper spine.

The cardiologist can also use **ultrasound echocardiography**, which uses sonar the way bats and dolphins do, to create an image of the heart on a screen. Sound waves that are much too high-pitched for humans to hear are bounced off different parts of the heart from different positions to give an accurate picture of the shape and movement of the heart valves, chambers, and walls.

TREATING CARDIOVASCULAR PROBLEMS

Today's doctors can choose from more than 100 different medications to treat patients with cardiovascular problems. Digitalis, for example, is a plant extract that has been used for over 200 years to help the heart pump better. Small amounts of nitroglycerin, which is used to make explosives, can relieve angina pain. This drug works by widening the blood vessels so that blood can flow more freely.

Other medications help lower the blood pressure, lower cholesterol levels in the blood, control the heartbeat rhythm, prevent deposits from building up in arteries, and help prevent clots from forming inside blood vessels. Doctors can inject drugs shortly after a heart attack to dissolve blood clots in the coronary arteries, and use medications to help seal up the hole in the heart septum of some newborn babies. It has even been found that taking half an aspirin a day greatly reduces the chance of a heart attack.

To clear a blocked coronary artery, the doctor can insert a tiny tube through the blood vessels and inject an anticoagulant to break up the clot. Or the heart surgeon may open the artery and try to remove the deposits that are clogging it. This procedure is called endarterectomy. In balloon **angioplasty** a catheter with a tiny balloon at the tip is slipped through the vessels to the clogged area. Then the balloon is inflated, pushing out the artery walls so that blood can flow freely. In laser angioplasty a catheter with a laser at the tip is pushed through the blood vessels until it reaches the blocked artery. The doctor then uses the laser to melt the fatty deposit as if it were butter. In **coronary bypass surgery**, doctors take a vein from a patient's leg and sew it onto the aorta to "bypass," or go around, the clogged artery.

When the body's pacemaker doesn't send impulses at the proper rhythm, a battery-operated artificial pacemaker can be inserted. It delivers carefully timed electric shocks that cause the heart to contract regularly.

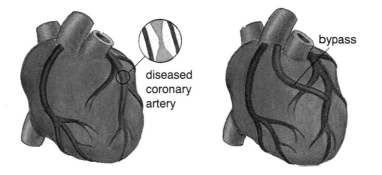

diseased coronary artery

bypass

A balloon pump is sometimes used to help an ailing heart pump more efficiently until the patient is ready for heart surgery. A balloon is pushed into the aorta at the end of a catheter, and helium is pumped in and out of it to make it expand and contract.

Doctors can fix many heart problems by open-heart surgery. Surgeons can sew up abnormal openings in hearts, or rearrange deformed hearts so that they work properly. Artificial valves made of plastic or metal can replace defective heart valves. Open-heart surgery would not be possible without the heart-lung machine, which filters, warms, and oxygenates the patient's blood while the doctors operate. Tubes inserted into blood vessels carry blood out of the body to the machine and then back again.

If the heart is so damaged that it can't be repaired, it may be replaced with one from someone who has just died. This operation, called a heart transplant, was first performed in 1967 by Dr. Christiaan Barnard in South Africa. But the body attacks the "foreign" cells in the new heart. Powerful drugs that suppress the immune system must be taken for the rest of the patient's life to prevent destruction of the transplanted heart.

There are not enough hearts available for transplants. Researchers have made progress toward developing a completely artificial heart, but much remains to be done.

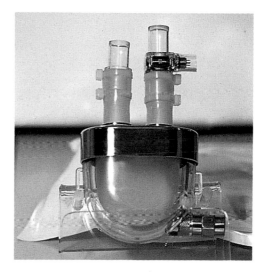

A modern artificial heart

KEEPING YOUR HEART HEALTHY

There are many risk factors that increase a person's chances of developing heart problems. We can't do anything about some of them, but many can be avoided. For most people, heart problems do not develop until middle age, but since they can begin while we're young, it's never too early to start thinking "heart-smart."

Diet is one of the most important factors that can lead to heart disease. In countries like the United States, where people eat diets that are high in fat and sugar, heart diseases are much more common. This type of diet can lead to high cholesterol levels in the blood. High cholesterol levels increase the chance of arteriosclerosis, which increases the chance of a heart attack.

Smoking cigarettes is another major risk factor for heart disease. Cigarette smoking cuts down the amount of oxygen reaching the heart muscles, raises the cholesterol level in the blood, increases the risk of blood clots, and can cause fibrillation.

Hypertension is the most common chronic disease, and it is believed to play a role in many heart attacks. Being overweight makes the heart work harder and also raises the blood pressure. Too much salt in the diet can also lead to hypertension in some people.

Stress is another important factor. Doctors have found that there are two basic types of people. "Type A" personalities are competitive and impatient. "Type B" people are more relaxed and easygoing. Type A people seem to be more prone to heart attacks. They need to learn how to deal with stress and how to relax.

Lack of exercise is also a very important risk factor. Exercise makes the heart stronger and able to do more with less work. It also helps to lower the weight and the blood pressure, and it decreases the type of cholesterol that is deposited in artery walls. Regular exercise can also help to relieve

*These young people at tennis camp
participate in a regular exercise program.*

stress. Running, bicycling, jumping rope, and swimming are good exercises for strengthening your cardiovascular system. They are called **aerobic exercises** because they make your heart and lungs work hard.

Your heart keeps on going, beat after beat, pumping life-giving oxygen and nutrients to the trillions of cells in your body. Keeping your heart and circulatory system healthy will help to keep your whole body healthy.

GLOSSARY

adrenaline—a hormone produced by the adrenal glands that works through the pacemaker to speed up the heartbeat rate.

aerobic exercise—exercise that makes the heart and lungs work hard.

agglutination—clumping; the combining of red blood cells into a solid mass, due to a reaction between antigens (agglutinogens) on the cell surface and antibodies (agglutinins) in the plasma.

AIDS—acquired immune deficiency syndrome, a disease caused by HIV, a virus that attacks blood cells including the T cells that help B cells make antibodies.

allergy—a reaction of the body to harmless foreign substances, such as plant pollens, as though they were invading germs.

anemia—a lack of sufficient red blood cells.

aneurysm—a weak spot in a blood vessel that may balloon out and burst.

angina pectoris—chest pain due to insufficient blood supply to the heart.

angiogram—X rays showing the movement of an injected dye through blood vessels and heart chambers.

angioplasty—opening of a clogged artery.

angiotensin—a blood pressure-raising hormone produced in the blood under the action of the kidney hormone renin.

antibodies—proteins that attack invading germs and foreign chemicals.

antigens—chemicals recognized as foreign to the body; they stimulate the production of antibodies that react with them very specifically.

antitoxins—antibodies against bacterial poisons.

aorta—the largest artery in the body; connected to the left ventricle.

arrhythmia—abnormal heartbeat.

arterioles—the smallest arteries.

arteriosclerosis—hardening of the arteries due to the buildup of fatty deposits (atherosclerosis), to which minerals are added.

artery—a blood vessel that carries blood away from the heart.

atrioventricular (A-V) node—a portion of the heart muscle that relays the electrical impulse that stimulates contraction from the atria to the ventricles.

atrium—the upper chamber of each side of the heart. (Plural: atria.)

autoimmune response—a mistaken attack of the immune system on body cells.

basophils—white blood cells that are involved in inflammation and healing.

B cells—lymphocytes that make antibodies.

blood—a red liquid that is carried by blood vessels through the body.

blood pressure—the pressure exerted by the blood on the walls of the blood vessels through which it is pumped.

blood vessels—tubes that carry blood between the heart and all parts of the body.

capillary—a tiny, thin-walled blood vessel connecting an artery or arteriole with a vein or venule.

carbon dioxide—a waste product formed when cells use fats or sugars for energy.

cardiac arrest—stopping of the heartbeat.

cardiac muscle—the heart muscle (myocardium).

cardiologist—a doctor specializing in heart disease.

cardiovascular—pertaining to the heart and blood vessels.

clot—a gellike, thickened lump formed from blood proteins that are trapped blood cells.

coagulation—blood clotting; the formation of a semisolid gel.

Cooley's anemia—a hereditary disorder that occurs among people of Mediterranean descent; similar to sickle-cell anemia.

coronary arteries—arteries that supply blood to the heart muscle.

coronary bypass surgery—grafting of a vein from the leg into the coronary circulation to bypass clogged vessels.

CPR (cardiopulmonary resuscitation)—a combination of mouth-to-mouth breathing and pressing on the chest, used as first aid after a heart attack.

deoxygenated blood—blood that carries very little oxygen.

diastole—the relaxing part of the heartbeat cycle.

diastolic pressure—the blood pressure when the heart is relaxing.

electrocardiograph (EKG or ECG)—a device that records the electrical activity of the heart. The record is called an electrocardiogram.

embolus—a blood clot formed inside a vein; embolism—the plugging of a blood vessel by an embolus that has broken loose and travels through the bloodstream, stopping the flow of blood to the part of the body supplied by that blood vessel and its branches.

endocarditis—inflammation of the endocardium.

endocardium—the inner lining of the heart.

eosinophils—white blood cells that detoxify foreign substances.

erythrocyte—a red blood cell.

erythropoietin—a kidney hormone that increases the production of red blood cells.

fibrin—a protein in the form of long, sticky fibers; formed from fibrinogen.

fibrinogen—a blood plasma protein that helps blood to clot.

foramen ovale—an opening between the two atria, present before birth.

formed elements—the blood cells.

gamma globulin—the fraction of blood containing antibodies against disease germs.

gangrene—death of cells in a part of the body to which circulation is cut off.

glomerulus—a tangle of capillaries that is part of the nephron (the filtering unit of the kidney).

glucose—a simple sugar, the body's main energy fuel.

granulocytes—a group of white blood cells with a grainy texture; includes eosinophils, basophils, and neutrophils.

heartbeat—a cycle of contraction and relaxation by the heart muscle, pumping blood into the arteries.

heart murmur—hissing sound heard between the sounds of the heartbeat.

hemoglobin—a red pigment that can combine with oxygen; it gives red blood cells their color.

hemophilia—a hereditary disorder in which the blood does not clot properly.

hemorrhage—heavy bleeding.

hemorrhoids—varicose veins in the rectal wall.

hormones—chemical messengers that help to control and coordinate body functions.

hypertension—high blood pressure.

immunity—a state of protection against particular disease germs due to the presence of antibodies or specially sensitized lymphocytes.

infectious mononucleosis—a viral disease causing increased production of larger-than-normal white blood cells.

inflammation—redness and swelling provoked by chemicals released by damaged cells.

jugular vein—the major vein in the neck.

leukemia—a form of cancer in which white blood cell production in the bone marrow goes out of control.

leukocyte—a white blood cell.

lipids—fatty chemicals, such as fats and cholesterol.

lymph—a clear, watery fluid that drains from body tissues into lymph capillaries.

lymphatic duct—the lymphatic that empties into a vein on the right side of the heart. It drains a smaller part of the body than the thoracic duct.

lymphatics—veinlike vessels that carry lymph.

lymphatic system—a network of vessels that carry lymph and return it to the blood circulation.

lymph nodes—swellings along the lymphatic system that contain germ filters and produce lymphocytes.

lymphocytes—white blood cells that defend against germs and foreign substances; some produce antibodies.

macrophages—large white blood cells; a form of monocytes.

mitral valve—a two-flap structure controlling the opening between the left atrium and left ventricle.

monocytes—white blood cells that attack and eat invading germs.

myocardial infarction—heart attack; death of part of the heart muscle due to blockage of its blood supply.

myocarditis—inflammation of the heart muscle.

myocardium—the heart muscle (cardiac muscle).

neutrophils—white blood cells that attack and eat invading germs.

oxygenated blood—oxygen-rich blood.

oxyhemoglobin—hemoglobin that has combined with oxygen.

pericarditis—inflammation of the pericardium.

pericardium—a sac enclosing the heart.

phlebitis—inflammation of a vein.

placenta—a structure on the inner surface of the womb in which gas exchange between the mother's blood and that of the developing fetus takes place.

plasma—the liquid part of blood, which remains after the formed elements are removed.

platelet factor—a substance released from damaged platelets that starts the chain of chemical reactions forming a blood clot.

platelets—blood cell fragments that help blood to clot; also called thrombocytes.

pulmonary arteries—the two branches of the pulmonary trunk that lead to the lungs.

pulmonary circulation—the loops of blood vessels leading from the heart to the lungs and back.

pulmonary trunk—the artery leading from the right ventricle.

pulse—the rhythmic beating produced by contractions of the arteries that can be felt at various places where arteries pass close to the skin surface.

red blood cells—disklike cells containing hemoglobin, which carry oxygen in the bloodstream; also called erythrocytes.

renal arteries—arteries carrying blood to the kidneys.

renin—an enzyme produced in the kidneys that activates angiotensin, a blood hormone that raises blood pressure.

rheumatic fever—an autoimmune illness that may develop after a strep throat infection, causing thickening and scarring of heart valves.

Rh factor—a red blood cell antigen separate from the ABO system.

semilunar valves—half-moon-shaped valves that control the flow of blood from ventricles to arteries.

septum—a partition, such as the one that divides the two sides of the heart.

sickle-cell anemia—a hereditary disorder in which misshapen red blood cells can clump and plug up blood vessels or rupture; it occurs mainly among people of African descent.

sinoatrial (S-A) node—the pacemaker: a portion of the heart muscle on the right atrium whose rhythmic contractions set the heartbeat rate.

sinusoids—greatly enlarged veins that act as blood reservoirs.

sphygmomanometer—an instrument used to measure blood pressure.

spleen—a spongy mass of lymphoid tissue that filters out germs, produces white blood cells, and acts as a blood reservoir.

stethoscope—a device that magnifies the sound of the heartbeat.

stress EKG—a recording of the heart's electrical activity made during exertion such as pedaling a stationary bike.

stroke—cutoff of the blood supply to a part of the brain, resulting in death of brain cells and loss of speech or other functions.

systemic circulation—the network of blood vessels carrying blood through all parts of the body (except for those blood vessels going to and from the lungs).

systole—the contracting part of the heartbeat cycle.

systolic pressure—the blood pressure when the heart is contracting.

T cells—lymphocytes that kill invading germs, seek out and destroy cancer cells, or control immune processes.

thoracic duct—the major lymphatic that empties into a vein close to the heart on the left.

thrombocytes—blood platelets.

thrombus—a blood clot; thrombosis—plugging of a blood vessel by a thrombus formed inside it.

tricuspid valve—a three-flap structure controlling the opening between the right atrium and right ventricle.

ultrasound echocardiography—the use of high-frequency sound waves bounced off heart structures to show heart structures and their movements.

umbilical cord—a ropelike connection between a developing fetus and its mother; the cord contains the umbilical blood vessels that carry nutrients to the fetus and remove its waste products.

universal donors—people with type O blood.

vaccination—the use of weakened or killed germs or other antigens to stimulate immunity against a disease.

valves—structures that control the flow of blood in the heart or in veins; lymphatics also have valves, which control the flow of lymph.

varicose veins—swollen veins caused by pooling of blood due to poorly functioning valves.

vascular—pertaining to the blood vessels.

vein—a blood vessel that carries blood toward the heart.

vena cava—one of the two largest veins, which empty into the heart. (Plural: venae cavae.)

ventricle—the thick-walled muscular lower chamber of each side of the heart.

ventricular fibrillation—a condition in which the heart quivers rapidly instead of contracting as a single unit and does not pump blood.

venules—the smallest veins.

white blood cells—colorless, irregularly shaped cells that are involved in the body's defenses against disease; also called leukocytes.

TIMELINE

B.C.

2650   Imhotep (Egyptian) felt the pulse to monitor heart action.

350   Aristotle (Greek) thought the heart contained the soul but observed chick embryo heart beating and named the aorta.

300   Erasistratos (Greek) observed arteries and veins.

160   Galen (Roman) thought the heart was a source of heat, blood flowed back and forth like tides, and the liver was the center of the circulatory system.

A.D.

early 1600s   William Harvey (English) discovered that the heart works as a pump sending blood in a one-way flow through the circulatory system.

1660s   Marcello Malpighi (Italian) discovered and named capillaries.

1660s   Antonie van Leeuwenhoek (Dutch) observed red blood cells in a tadpole.

mid-1700s   Stephen Hales (English) described blood pressure.

late 1800s   Elie Metchnikoff (Russian) discovered white blood cells.

1901   Karl Landsteiner (Austrian) discovered ABO blood types.

1903   Willem Einthoven (Dutch) developed an electrocardiograph .

1952   F. John Lewis (American) performed the first successful open-heart surgery.

1954   John Gibbon (American) used a heart-lung machine to take the place of the heart and lungs during an operation.

1957   Willem Kolff (American) implanted artificial hearts in dogs.

1960s   Adrian Kantorowicz (American) developed a battery-powered pacemaker for patients whose hearts weren't beating properly.

1967   Christiaan Barnard (South African) performed first human heart transplant.

1982   William DeVries (American) implanted a Jarvik-7 artificial heart that kept a human patient alive for 112 days.

1987   Use of "clot busters" streptokinase and TPA (tissue plasminogen activator) to dissolve clots and reduce damage after a heart attack. Discovery of a heart hormone, atrial natriuretic factor.

INDEX